MONSTER MANUAL

MONSTER MANUAL

A Complete Guide to Your Favorite Creatures

by Erich Ballinger

Lerner Publications Company • Minneapolis

This edition first published 1994 by Lerner Publications Company. All English language rights reserved.

This book is available in two editions:
Library binding by Lerner Publications Company
Soft cover by First Avenue Editions, 1996.
241 First Avenue North
Minneapolis, MN 55401

ISBN: 0-8225-0722-6 (lib. bdg.)
ISBN: 0-8225-9771-3 (pbk.)

Original edition copyright © 1989 by Verlag Carl Ueberreuter under the title, *ABC für Monsterfans: ein Leselexikon.* Translated from the German by Catherine Kerkhoff-Saxon. Translation copyright © 1994 by Lerner Publications Company. Additional text and illustrations copyright © 1994 by Lerner Publications Company.

Library of Congress Cataloging-in-Publication Data

Ballinger, Erich.
    [ABC für Monsterfans. English]
    Monster manual : a complete guide to your favorite creatures / by Erich Ballinger.
        p. cm.
    Includes bibliographical references and index.
    ISBN 0-8225-0722-6
    1. Monsters—Dictionaries—Juvenile literature. I. Title.
GR825.B2518 1994
001.9′44′03—dc20   93-34219

Manufactured in the United States of America
2 3 4 5 6 7 - MA - 01 00 99 98 97 96

INTRODUCTION

Did I hear you right? Did you say you enjoy the jitters and the feeling of prickly goose bumps? You like to be so scared out of your wits that even the sound of your own breath makes you shudder? You live for the nameless terror that grabs your heart on sultry moonlit nights? Then welcome to our magic circle, our exclusive club. Welcome, friends who love what they fear—welcome, Monster Fans!

In our book, *Monster Manual,* you'll find everything you've always wanted to know about monsters, as well as some things you'd rather not know. That's all right, for we fans of the bizarre never fail to look even the most terrifying truth straight in the eye.

To use *Monster Manual,* you should first know that:

 the entries are in alphabetical order;

 words are easier to look up if you check the top corner of the pages (there you'll find the first and last entries of each page spread);

 a word in **bold type** means that if you want to know more about this word, look it up—it's another entry;

 at the end of the book is an alphabetical index, which lists many monster-related words found in the book.

You don't have to read the book in an orderly manner, however. You can just wickedly paw through the book, monsterlike, and pick out a topic that happens to fit your bloodthirsty state of mind.

So, Monster Fans, off you go—into your snuggly tight, moldy coffins! But leave the lid open a crack, so that the flickering flame of a candle may illuminate the gloriously spooky pages of this book!

A

"Teddy bears are out, monsters are in."
—*TRENDSETTER MAGAZINE*

ALIENS

JOHN ALLEN! STOP ALL THAT NONSENSE ABOUT ALIENS!

It looks like the innards of a butchered cow. Sticky, slimy, and eight feet long. It meows like a cat and eats humans. It bleeds green blood. It comes from the farthest reaches of the universe: from Mars, from Pluto, from Planet X, or from the depths of the Andromeda nebula. It is the scout for an invasion unit of similar creatures who want to colonize the earth and enslave its inhabitants. Is human life as we know it beyond all hope?

Have no fear, earthlings! This creature is merely one of hundreds of extraterrestrial monsters populating movies and television, an "alien." In a general sense, "alien" means foreign or unfamiliar; here, in particular, an alien is a being from outer space. Not all aliens are bad: some good aliens warn humankind of war, nuclear bomb tests, and environmental pollution. With their outstanding intelligence and technological wizardry, they are quite helpful when it comes to the destiny of our planet. Two representatives of this category are **E.T.**, and Klaatu, from *The Day the Earth Stood Still* (1951).

Bad aliens are more common, however. They are all ugly and unappetizing and starving for…SMACK, SLURP, YUM, YUM… human flesh.

These classic movies, most of which are available on video, contain alien characters: *Enemy from Space* (1957), *The Creeping Unknown* (1956), *The Thing (From Another World)* (1951), *Invasion of the Body Snatchers* (1956), and *The Blob* (1958).

DAVROS

THE THING

GORN

Monster Fans know that these movies are fantasy, manufactured to bring us two hours of undisturbed sweet horror. But many people don't seem to realize this, as the following true story shows:

In 1938, on **Halloween,** the CBS studios in New York City broadcast a radio play by Orson Welles (adapted from a novel by H. G. Wells) called *The War of the Worlds.* The broadcast sounded extremely realistic. Without warning, dance music was interrupted and the radio announcer declared that an observatory had reported large explosions on Mars. The music continued, then again a speaker interrupted with a special report: A huge flaming object had fallen on a farm in Grover's Mill, New Jersey. He advised people to stay tuned and more information would follow. More music. And then came the frightening announcement: Strange creatures had deboarded the object, shooting heat rays at the crowd of observers. At least 40 people lay dead!

The station's lines were blocked by hysterical callers. People stormed the streets and blocked traffic. Others rounded up their families, hoping to get out of town by car. Traffic came to a standstill. Total panic.... And this whole situation was caused by a make-believe story about a Martian landing!

A good number of intelligent people believe in the reality of alien life. Erich von Däniken, a Swiss writer and pseudo-archaeologist, claims with all seriousness in his books that aliens visited the earth thousands of years ago. The impression the aliens made on the people of the Stone Age can be seen in their legends, myths, and religions, von Däniken says. Scientists smirk condescendingly, yet von Däniken's books sell by the millions.

By the way—von Däniken believes that the next visit by aliens will take place in this century. Have you got your laser beam disintegration pistol loaded and cocked?

B

(Greek, basiliskos *= little king)*

BASILISK

Nothing's easier than breeding this legendary monster: take a yolkless rooster egg, place it in a dung heap, and make a toad sit on the egg until the egg hatches. Raising a basilisk to maturity is, however, more difficult: its beastly, stinking breath destroys all living things within a radius of 30 feet, and its touch turns everything to dust. And don't let it look in a mirror— the sight of a basilisk is so repulsive that it's deadly not only for humans, but also for the basilisk itself.

In ancient Greece and Rome, and during the Middle Ages (about A.D. 500 to 1500), people actually believed in the existence of this monster. Sometime during the 15th century in Basel, Switzerland, a rooster was brought to trial. The charge: laying an egg from which a basilisk hatched. The verdict: guilty. The punishment: death by hanging. The city executioner lynched the rooster. It was evidently a quite effective measure. Since then, no basilisks have been spotted in or around Basel.

BOGEYMONSTER

The bogeymonster and the big bad wolf are monsters that caused us a lot of anxiety in early childhood. Although we now find them quite ridiculous, it was not so long ago that an adult threatened us with "Just you wait, if you don't do this or that, then the such-and-such will come and get you!" and we were terrified. But since nothing actually ever happened, we soon outgrew our belief in these monsters.

Such creations are so-called educational monsters, thought up to make little children eat their vegetables and learn their manners. But friends, do we really need a bogeymonster to get us to eat our spinach, and a big bad wolf to make sure we learn to say "please" and "thank you"? Let's hand these old-fashioned, shabby monsters over to the trash collectors, who can dump them where they can do no more harm!

BOSCH, HIERONYMUS

A creature with a horse's skull, in knight's armor and a garish green cape, plays the harp. This ghastly musician sits upon a two-legged monster wearing wooden clogs, which resembles a plucked goose with a rat's head.

A huge rat wades through murky water. A woman rides its back—she is part tree, part fish. She clenches a dead child in her knobby, gnarled arms.

In the flaming-red sky, an egg soars past, wings spread wide. It carries a bloated toad, armed with helmet and lance.

These horrible visions are only a few of many from a painting by Hieronymus Bosch (about 1450–1516). Bosch was a Dutch artist who painted pictures of monsters and other infernal  scenes. His pictures put everything ever produced in Hollywood to shame. He is the unrivaled master of all monster makers.

Yet Bosch's contemporaries viewed his paintings differently than we view our movie monsters. Each scary figure and gruesome situation had a specific symbolic meaning that was understood by the people of the Middle Ages. His paintings hung in churches, where they cautioned people against a life of sin; they illustrated vividly the torments awaiting an evildoer in Hell.

Even if we don't have the ability to read his paintings as stories, this shouldn't stop us from admiring Bosch's monster world with a mixture of repulsion and fascination. His pictures hang in museums in Berlin, Frankfurt, Geneva, Lisbon, London, Madrid, Munich, New York, Paris, Philadelphia, Rotterdam, São Paulo, Venice, Vienna, and Washington, D.C. If you happen to be in one of these places, be sure to take a look at his paintings. You don't mind a few sleepless nights, do you?

FOR 100 YEARS, ALL HAS BEEN PEACEFUL IN THE DARK SWAMP. THAT IS, UNTIL NOW. . . .

OH NO!

CONTINUED ON P. 14

C

"Evil is the root of all monsters."
—GREEK PHILOSOPHER

CALIGARI

CESARE

Right after World War I, in 1919, a film was released that protested against the horrors of war: *Das Kabinett des Dr. Caligari* (*The Cabinet of Dr. Caligari*).

Dr. Caligari is the owner of a sideshow booth and director of an insane asylum. The instrument of his devilish intentions—Cesare, the sleepwalker—slumbers in a coffin and obeys Caligari, lacking any willpower of his own. Nightly, Caligari sends him out to commit atrocious murders. Like a soldier at war, Cesare obeys the commands of his master. He doesn't think. He doesn't feel. He acts. He kills. And despite his eerie appearance and crimes, it is not Cesare who is the monster, but the mad director of the insane asylum.

Caligari is not only an excellent thriller, it is also a milestone in the history of cinema—a classic.

The entire movie was shot inside a studio. The sky, landscapes, and backdrops were designed by Berlin artists. In one scene, you see Cesare's flight over the rooftops as a nightmarelike vision: grotesque forms, crooked chimneys, gaping, ominous windows, streaks of light flashing through the shadowy scenery like saber cuts. Cesare himself has been made up with paint and moves along contortedly, as if to mimic the bizarre lines of the scenery. This movie laid the foundation for expressionistic film. It's an absolute must for all gourmets of the grotesque.

Director: Robert Wiene
Script: Kurt Mayer, Hans Janowitz
Sets, costumes: the artists' association Der Sturm (The Storm)

CHANEY, LON

Lon (Alonso) Chaney (1883–1930), the unsurpassed Grand Monster of silent horror movies, was literally born to be a silent movie actor. His parents were deaf and mute, and he could only communicate with them through body language. This experience proved to be a great training ground for his later film work.

Chaney was his own **makeup** artist as well. With hidden wires and cleverly mounted artificial parts, he could alter his face to such a degree that viewers did not recognize him from film to film. Once, after a showing of one of Chaney's movies, a huge spider crawled through the theater's aisles. Some people reacted by backing away fearfully. Others, more daring, wanted to scrunch it. A joker cried out: "Don't step on it! It may be Chaney!"

At the zenith of his fame, Chaney was struck with cancer of the larynx. The great silent film star was fated to silence, up to his death at age 47.

CHANEY   CHANEY   CHANEY   CHANEY (?)

Chaney's son, Lon Chaney, Jr. (1905–1973), kept his father's monster tradition alive and thriving. He played the first werewolf ever, now a classic role as well (see: **Phantom of the Opera, Quasimodo, Karloff, werewolves**).

GLORP, THE TERROR OF ALL HUMANITY, RISES OUT OF THE MURKY WATERS.

GURBLE GURBLE

SLURP

NO NOT THIS AGAIN!

CONTINUED ON P.18

COMIC BOOK MONSTERS

HELLO, FANS! HERE WE ARE, THE MONSTERS FROM THE PAGES OF YOUR FAVORITE COMICS.

BLACKART

WE DON'T WANT TO BE TOO WORDY HERE. LONG SPEECHES ARE NOT OUR THING.

THE LIZARD

HARD FACTS AND HOT ACTION ARE MORE ALONG OUR LINE.

POK

SOLOMON GRUNDY

THERE ARE ABSOLUTELY ZILLIONS OF US COMIC BOOK MONSTERS...

ARKON

...IN ALL COUNTRIES ON EARTH...

SPIDER-MAN

* AND IN ALL LANGUAGES.

TARS TARKAS

WE COME FROM THE OUTER REACHES OF SPACE...

TOAD

...FROM THE GREATEST DEPTHS OF THE EARTH...

TKTK

....FROM AGES AND AGES AGO...

NERGON

... AND FROM THE DISTANT FUTURE...

IRON MAN

...FROM IMAGINARY WORLDS AND FROM DREAMS.

MONSTER OF THE LOST LAGOON

NUCLEAR ACCIDENTS TURNED US INTO MONSTERS...

BLASTAAR

...BLACK MAGIC GAVE US SUPERNATURAL POWERS...

ZOM

...OR MAD SCIENTISTS CREATED US TO TERRORIZE HUMANITY.

ROBROX

SOME OF US ARE GOOD...

THE VISION

...SOME OF US ARE BAD, AND THERE ARE THOSE...

MR. FEAR

...WHO CAN'T MAKE UP THEIR MINDS.

SILVER SURFER

IF OUR READERS DON'T LIKE US...

RED SKULL

WE END UP IN THE PUBLISHER'S DARKEST, DEEPEST, FILE DRAWER. DONE FOR! ZAPPED!

BUT OUR WORST ENEMIES ARE THOSE WHO SAY THAT COMICS ARE FOR ILLITERATES— THAT COMICS ARE TRASH.

JINNI DEVIL

MUDSLINGERS, THAT'S WHAT THEY ARE! BUT IT'S NOT A PROBLEM REALLY...

THE THING

...BECAUSE FOR THEM, IT'S CLOBBERING TIME!

FLOMP!

STOMPING OFF LOUDLY, THE MONSTER SETS OUT

IN SEARCH OF A VICTIM.

(CONTINUED ON P. 25)

D

"Oldies but moldies…"
—AN EXPRESSION COINED IN THE 1930s

DINOSAURS

Dinosaurs don't really belong in this book, because they're not monsters. Dinosaurs, as you know, are actual creatures that lived somewhere between 225 million to 65 million years ago. Dinosaurs are included in this book simply because they are so beautiful: So beautifully ghastly. So beautifully large. So beautifully brutal. And because there are some misunderstandings to be straightened out here—and well-informed Monster Fans should know the facts.

The last dinosaur died millions of years before the first human being inhabited the earth. Battles between cave dwellers and dinosaurs exist in some movies, novels, and comics, but they are pure nonsense. No matter how wonderful it would be, we have to face it: dinosaurs have long been extinct.

Dinosaurs came in many shapes and sizes. Not all dinosaurs were as tall as an Ultrasaurus (55 feet), or as long as a Seismosaurus (150 feet), or as heavy as a Brachiosaurus (50 tons). A full-grown Compsognathus was just the size of a hen.

Some dinosaurs were meat-eaters with more than 1,000 teeth; others were peaceful plant-eaters. Some could have run faster than Carl Lewis (100 meters in 9.86 seconds). Some were clumsy and slow.

ALLOSAURUS

STEGOSAURUS

Dinosaurs in movies are usually pure fantasy. They often resemble a crossbreed of a Tarbosaurus, Pentaceratops, and Kentrosaurus. Most of these dinosaur-monster films are available on video: *Godzilla, King of the Monsters* (1956), *Gorgo* (1961), *Valley of Gwangi* (1969), *Gigantis, the Fire Monster* (1959), *Dinosaurus!* (1960), *The Last Dinosaur* (1977), *Jurassic Park* (1993).

Some incredibly realistic dinosaurs have been created with new special-effects techniques (as seen in the dinosaur models of *Jurassic Park*). But before these innovations, some movie directors used live lizards as dinosaurs. They glued scales and spines to the lizards' bodies and made them fight against members of their own species. These movies were shot in slow motion. Film of the human actors was copied onto the films later, making the lizards look very large and the humans look very small. This method was cheaper than animating large models with stop-motion photography, and it produced a more natural effect than could otherwise be achieved at the time. Luckily, the American Society for the Prevention of Cruelty to Animals stepped in, and this shooting procedure was forbidden.

STOP-MOTION PHOTOGRAPHY

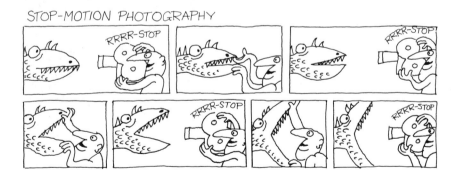

DRACULA

Who doesn't know, love, and fear that heartless count from Transylvania, that superstar of all **vampires?** Compared to him, his colleagues seem quite bland—they lack the proper bite.

Yet, how many of you know who invented Count Dracula? Have you ever heard of Bram Stoker?

In his early career as a writer, Bram Stoker (1847–1912) had not been very successful. But at the turn of the 20th century, when Stoker was 50 years old, he created a masterpiece: *Dracula.*

For this book, Stoker carried out extensive research. Teeth clenched, he studied the gruesome settings for his novel with utmost care: cemeteries under the light of a full moon, tombs by candlelight, dockyards in fog, church ruins during a thunderstorm. Stoker never actually visited Transylvania, but he absorbed facts about this mysterious Romanian region from travelogs, maps,

BELA LUGOSI

cookbooks, and ferry schedules. Stoker's brother, a surgeon, supplied him with the necessary anatomical details and information about blood.

The effort was worth it. Soaring batlike, Dracula rose to immortal fame. His creator stayed earthbound and died in 1912, a natural death (see: **Nosferatu**).

The film industry has also played a large part in Dracula's popularity. Ever since the book came out, movie after movie has been released in which blood spurts across the screen as the thirsty count thrusts his fangs into a silky, naked throat.

Over and over again, stakes have been thrust through Drac's chest, his head severed from his body—finished, dead, done for, moviegoers like to think after each film. But then there he is again in the next movie—pale, but still with a soft spot for a bloody snack. Consecrated wafers, crosses, and garlic don't help. Dracula just plain refuses to bite the dust for good.

Among the many actors who have played Dracula, two did so especially well:

Bela Lugosi (1882–1956) was a Hungarian immigrant to Hollywood. His aristocratic countenance, his clownlike, devilish **makeup,** and his strong Hungarian accent made him particularly popular with American audiences in the 1931 movie *Dracula.* Yet when his style went out of fashion, he wasn't given much to sink his teeth into. He died a poor and embittered man. As he had wished, he was buried in Dracula's red-and-black satin cape.

Fresh blood was brought to vampire movies by the English actor Christopher Lee. He had to his advantage his great height, new biting techniques, and color film. (Blood has that special something in technicolor!) *Horror of Dracula* (1958) was the first in a series of vampire films starring Lee.

Hold on tight now, don't fall off your chair:

Dracula actually existed!

There was, in fact, more than one Dracula, for Dracula was the name of a Romanian family of noble descent. Vlad Dracula III seems to have been particularly diabolic. He was born in 1431 in Sighisoara, Romania, and was known to inflict atrocities on his enemies and subjects. For example, after one victorious battle, he skewered the Turks he had captured by the dozens. He was also said to have had fits of cannibalism. Of course, he wasn't a vampire, but he was certainly an inspiring model for Bram Stoker's *Dracula.*

Today, Dracula's legacy is in the clutches of the Romanian Tourist Office. You can visit Vlad Dracula's birthplace, the monastery in which he was educated, the sites of his massacres, and his castle, which looms 900 feet over the Arges River valley on steep walls of rock. Leading up to the castle are 1,400 steps. If you get all sticky and sweaty during the climb, the chilly, musty aura of horror that drifts from the ruins will cool you off. Several inns in the area serve dishes described by Stoker in his novel. And I do hope you have nothing against garlic.

If you have read the entries **Dracula, Nosferatu,** and **vampires** with care, you have earned the title "Certified Bloody-Minded Vampire and Dracula Expert." Congratulations! Test your wisdom on the following text. It tells part of the Dracula story, but the author (truly *not* an expert) has made 10 horrendous slips. Find them and you may award yourself the Very Distinguished Medal of High Garlic!

...It was night. The new moon cast bizarre shadows on the lawn surrounding the old house. A dark figure stood near the bloodwort bush. It was Baron Dracula. A grimace passed over his suntanned face and his sharp incisors flashed dangerously. He spread his green plaid cape and flew, like a huge vulture, to an open window on the first floor. The Transiberian vampire snorted angrily when he saw the onions hanging there to ward off moths. Shaken by disgust and distaste, he pushed his way past these repulsive bulbs into the room. It was the bedchamber of Verena M., a college professor of mathematics and physics. Greedily, the vampire focused his bloodshot eyes on the open box of candies lying on the nightstand. He resisted the temptation. Later, for dessert, he would indulge in a tender chocolate-covered candy with a creamy hazelnut center. For the moment, however, he would concentrate on the main dish. Verena was breathing heavily, tossing and turning in her sleep, as if haunted by bad dreams. In the distance, a church clock struck one. The vampire leaned over the sleeping damsel, his fangs glistening. And then—yes—licking his chops, he bit his victim's big toe....

(See: Solutions on p. 140.)

HIS VICTIM IS A LITTLE GIRL WHO HAS BEEN SENT TO HER ROOM FOR THE EVENING.
(CONTINUED ON P.28)

DRAGONS

Dragons are international. Everywhere in the world where people tell stories, they tell about these serpentine, winged, fire-spitting monsters that look more or less like certain **dinosaurs.** A few scientists have an explanation for the worldwide popularity of dragons. It goes something like this:

Hundreds of millions of years ago, when dinosaurs ruled the world, the first mammals came into being—small ratlike omnivores.* They were our great-grandparents. The enormous impression made by gigantic dinosaurs on this little animal was imprinted forever on its brain and passed on to its great-grandchildren of today, human beings. This "memory of dinosaurs" is expressed in our legends and myths.

Naturally, this theory has not remained unchallenged.

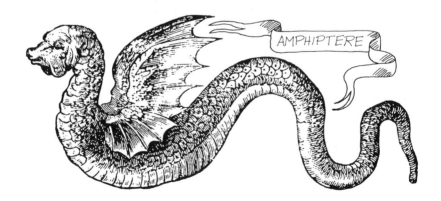

*animals that eat both vegetable and animal substances

Although dragons are popular in legends of both the West and East, the creatures do have their differences. Dragons of the Western world embody evil, live in caves, guard treasures, hold young maidens captive, and are usually slain by heroes. Dragons of the Eastern world are good, protect the gods, provide rain, and are responsible for good harvests. People worship them and celebrate festivals in their honor.

In addition, dragon specialists differentiate between fire, air, earth, and water dragons; legless wormlike dragons called lindworms (found only in the European Alps); and Uroboros (a dragon that bites itself in the tail and is a magic symbol for alchemists).

WATER DRAGON

If you attempt to measure your strength against a dragon and are victorious, don't forget: bathe yourself in its blood, and your skin will be impenetrable; eat its liver, and you'll understand the languages of all animals; bury its teeth, and armed soldiers loyal only to you will sprout from the earth.

MENACINGLY, GLORP PLANTS HIMSELF BEHIND THE UNSUSPECTING CHILD. (CONTINUED ON P. 47)

DRAWING MONSTERS

Before you begin drawing a monster, you should know one thing: drawing monsters is the easiest thing in the world. It's much, much easier than, for example, drawing a horse.

Let's say you draw a horse. If you show your horse to someone and say, "This is a horse," they are sure to say, "Yes, but...." And then they'll give you a whole lecture on the anatomy of a horse and the grace of this animal, and they'll probably throw in a nasty comment like, "Horses have hooves, not slippers."

Now draw a horse again, but don't try as hard as you did the first time. Show this picture to someone and say, "This is the Cuddlelidoo monster from the Kisskissian Swamp." If your art critic now says, "Yes, but...," ask your smart friend if he or she has ever seen a Cuddlelidoo. You'll never have heard a more wonderful silence!

The point is, a monster can look however you like. Seven eyes, a tail on its nose, and a thirteenth foot growing out of its ear. Who would dare claim that such a monster *doesn't* exist!?

Do you feel more courageous now? Do you dare to draw the feared Swarp from the Zuzuki Canyon? Good! Then do it! Throw this book aside and get to work!

And for the less courageous of you who would like a little help, *Monster Manual* proudly presents the first and only:

INSTANT MONSTER
DRAWING COURSE

Just follow the simple suggestions on the next two pages.

1. Splotch some ink or paint on a piece of paper. Let your imagination run wild, and you'll see the most marvelous of monsters in these weird forms. With the aid of a pen, you can help others to recognize your fantasy figures. For instance:

2. Try out your imagination on bizarre shadows and on crumpled and torn paper. With some practice, you will see hundreds of monstrous faces grinning your way.

   Below is a piece of crumpled tissue paper that has been photocopied. Can you see the monster? Copy your own monster, then help things along a bit with a pen.

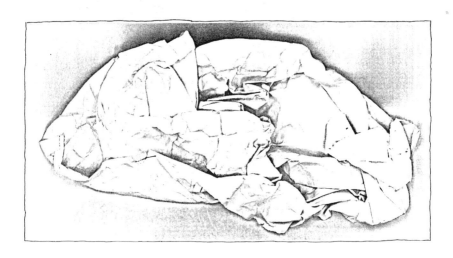

3. Find a photo of a handsome face. Add a few details with your pen, and cover up other things with white correction fluid or opaque white paint.

 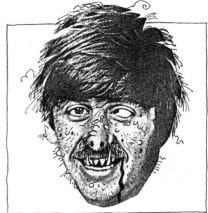

4. Cut two photos of two incredibly boring people from any old magazine. Combine them to make one face, and a quite alarming monster emerges:

5. The course is over. *Monster Manual* thanks all participants for their participation.

So you want to know if you've passed the course? Here's a test that never fails:

Draw a horse. Show it to someone and ask, "What do you see?"

a) Their answer is "A monster."
   You have passed with honors! Congratulations!
b) Their answer is "A horse."
   You have not learned a thing. Congratulations!
c) Some other answer is given.
   You have participated. Congratulations!

E

"A hair-raising affair."
—ANNOUNCEMENT FOR A MONSTER BENEFIT

EEEEEEEEEEEK!

"Eeeeeeeeeeek" (shrill and loud) is the frightfully common sound made by a half-naked woman as she dangles helplessly in the claws of some gruesome monster. And usually there is a heroic man at hand, ready to liberate her and save the day.

Fans, isn't this setup getting boring? What a cliché! How about telling the story this way for once: A half-naked man dangles helplessly in the claws of a gruesome monster. Standing by is a heroic woman ready to liberate him.

Or this way: A half-naked monster dangles helplessly in the claws of a gruesome woman, and a male hero flees.

Or...? The possibilities go on and on. In fact, by scrambling the words *half-naked, gruesome, heroic, man, woman, monster, liberate,* and *flee,* you can describe up to 72 different cinematic situations—a soothing activity when sleeplessness hits after a monster film.

E.T.

E.T. is not a name, exactly. E.T. stands for "Extra-Terrestrial." E.T. is a quite lovable monster from outer space, probably the most well-known of all **aliens.** E.T. holds a special place in the hearts of all Monster Fans.

E.T. The Extra-Terrestrial is a film by monster expert Steven Spielberg (who also directed or produced the movies *Jaws, Close Encounters of the Third Kind, Poltergeist, Gremlins,* and *Jurassic Park*). The story goes like this:

By mistake, a young alien is left behind on Earth by his companions. He has to struggle to survive. He's not classically handsome, but he's cute in a monstrous way: he's wrinkly and yellowish, with a big head and sparkling saucerlike eyes. He isn't strong, but he can bring dead flowers back to life and has telekinetic* powers. He is much more intelligent than we are. But he has a weakness for sweets, just like you and me.

*having the power to move objects without using physical strength

The story of E.T. may seem vaguely familiar to you. Director Steven Spielberg admits he got the idea from a book, a centuries-old bestseller. Do you know which one? To help you out, here's the movie's plot in a few words: E.T. comes from the heavens (in a spaceship) and is all alone in a hostile world. E.T. can perform miracles. He finds his followers in the oppressed (children), and is persecuted by the powerful (adults). Imprisonment and death follow, then resurrection and ascension. In addition, E.T. has super-natural intelligence, goodness, and a (telephone) connection to "above." Right! The movie has remarkable similarities to a famous story from the Bible.

Here are some facts about the film:

World Premiere:
May 25, 1982

Contributors:
 5 directors
11 producers, production supervisors, co-producers, production managers, and production coordinators
 3 business managers
 3 screenwriters and script supervisors
11 photography managers, camera operators, camera assistants, lighting technicians, and dolly* operators
27 composers, musicians, mixers, sound engineers, and editors
 1 gardener
 8 production designers, illustrators, set designers, construction coordinators, model builders, and painters
 5 editors and editing assistants
 1 animal trainer
24 E.T. designers and operators
62 specialists for animated shots

*a mobile platform for a camera

 5 prop handlers and prop constructors
 6 hairdressers, makeup artists, and wardrobe artists
 2 transportation coordinators
 1 teacher
16 medical advisers
15 actors in main roles
10 stuntmen and stuntwomen
 1 nurse

"Every good family has a few skeletons in its closet."
—FROM *THE BOOK OF MONSTROUSLY GOOD BREEDING*

FAMILY TREE

On clear nights when a full moon is brightly shining, sleepless Monster Fans anxiously ask themselves two questions: Where do monsters come from? And do they really exist?

Let's take the second question first. No, monsters don't really exist. Neither in the unexplored black lagoons of the Amazon, nor in the snowbound gorges of the Himalayas; neither in rotting coffins, nor in subterranean labs. Monsters are fiction, or make-believe. Monsters only exist in our heads—in our fantasies, dreams, wishes, and fears. So where do monsters come from? If we open a little door in our heads, the monsters stroll out, to be captured in legends, novels, movies, paintings, and books.

The family tree on the next two pages shows you the origins of monsters and how they can be divided and subdivided into groups. The monstrous fruits at the end of each branch are examples of many similar monsters in the same categories.

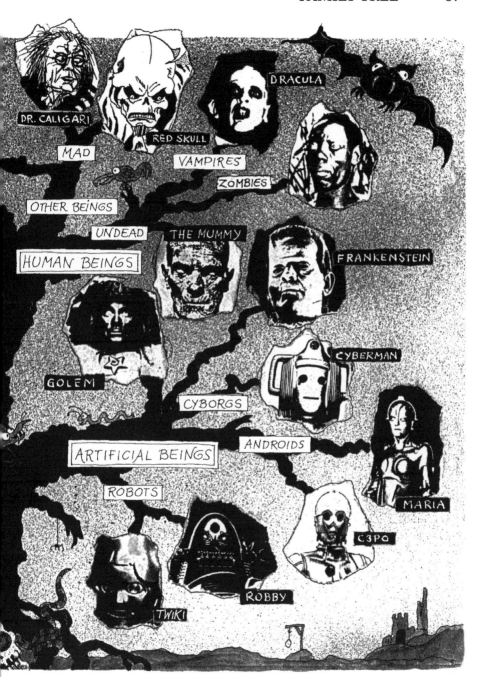

FEAR

Fear reveals itself in a variety of forms: we turn pale, our teeth chatter, we get **goose bumps** or jitters, our hearts pound, our stomachs churn, our breath becomes short. Fear can be unpleasant.

At the same time, fear is important. Fear helps us stay alive, for it's fear that keeps us from stepping out in front of a bus or a speeding train. People who fear too little die too soon. They are sometimes called heroes, sometimes fools.

It's certainly not a disgrace to be afraid of something, nor is it ridiculous. In fact, a trace of fear is absolutely necessary to enjoy monsters. No fear, no monsters—wouldn't that be a pity!

The test below doesn't measure how courageous you are—just whether or not you have the necessary amount of fear to be a true Monster Fan.

TEST YOUR FEAR

Check one box for each question!

The picture on the left shows:
- ☐ a) a battle between **King Kong** and **Godzilla** at dusk (2 points)
- ☐ b) flowers swaying gently in the breeze (4 points)
- ☑ c) an ink stain (5 points)

This man is saying:
- ☐ a) "Fee, fi, fo, fum, I smell the blood of an Englishman!" (1 point)
- ☐ b) "It's a pleasure to meet you!" (3 points)
- ☑ c) "I'm allergic to mosquito bites." (4 points)

In this situation, you would:
☐ a) offer the monster garlic (3 points)
☐ b) scream for help (2 points)
☑ c) ask the movie director for a
five-minute break (4 points)

Write the word *Dracula* on a piece
of paper.
☐ a) Your handwriting is shaky.
(1 point)
☑ b) Your handwriting is even and
flowing. (3 points)
☐ c) You spelled *Dracula* with a *T.*
(5 points)

Call a huge, strong bully an insulting
name.
☑ a) You wouldn't even dream of
doing that. (0 points)
☐ b) You did it and are now lying in
the hospital. (10 points)
☑ c) You dared to, but you're a good
sprinter. (3 points)

EVALUATION

6 to 10 points:
Hey, you're a born Monster Fan! You know the ins and outs of
enjoying horror and terror. Keep it up!

11 to 20 points:
You are a very realistic person. A little more imagination wouldn't
hurt. Yet there's still hope that one day you too will experience
the thrill and pleasure of **goose bumps.**

21 to 28 points:
You are a hopeless case—the born hero. If you make it to the age of 20, you could become a stuntperson. Advise your parents to take out life insurance on you.

THE FLY

It could happen to you or me too: While carrying out a seemingly harmless scientific experiment, a fly gets into your activated genetic matter transporter machine, and womp! There you are. Instead of your own head, you have the head of a fly. Between your huge compound eyes, two antennae have sprouted. Where your arms once were, you have thin, hairy legs ending in sticky, clawed feet. What's more, you are strangely attracted to the sweet smell of decayed potato peelings and rotten meat. Meanwhile, the poor fly buzzing around you has your head and your arms. You, whichever of the two you may now be—the fly head and thorax with the human legs, or—oh, never mind.

You must be thinking this whole mess is bound to end badly. And it does. In the movie *The Fly* (1958), and in its 1986 remake, both mutations come to tragic ends. So it pays to check before you flip the switch: Is your genetic matter transporter machine sealed up tight?

FRANKENSTEIN

First of all, we've got to settle something: Frankenstein's first name is Victor, he has a medical degree, and he is a mad scientist. He is the one who digs up limbs of corpses in cemeteries. He pieces these repulsive parts together in his lab to make an artificial being. And it is also he who brings this creation to life, using a bunch of complicated contraptions. The creature he produces is called *Dr. Frankenstein's monster,* and not *Frankenstein,* as those with little knowledge of monsters often assume. So, that settles that.

THE BOOK

Although we are most familiar with its incarnation on film, the story of Frankenstein was not conceived by a movie studio. It was the product of the imagination of a 19-year-old woman named Mary Wollstonecraft Shelley (1797–1851). And this, precisely, is how the story came to life:

For days it had been pouring, and fog hung low over the Swiss Alps. Tucked inside a chalet, a small group of English writers were sitting around a fireplace, drinking tea. They were quite bored. Perhaps, they thought, a volume of German horror stories would relieve the monotony. It did.

At the end of the reading, enthusiasm was running unusually high. Everyone agreed to try his or her own hand at a truly blood-curdling, unnerving thriller.

Mary Shelley went to bed late that evening, slept badly, and dreamt a particularly ugly dream. The next morning, she wrote it down in her diary. *Frankenstein* had been born.

Frankenstein's monster is repulsively ugly, but not at all mean. He loves humans and wants them to love him too. Clumsy and childlike, this hulking creature approaches person after person and tries to express his affection. They all have the same reaction. At the sight of his ugly face and giant size, they bolt in panic or reject his endearments, as if it were a matter of life or death. The monster can't understand why they treat him like they do. He feels quite isolated and lonely. He becomes sadder and sadder. He becomes bitter. He becomes mean. The physical monster has now become an emotional monster as well.

THE MOVIE

This massive, clunky monster stomping across the screen has long held our love and fear. How impressively he stiffly thuds along, the ground quaking beneath him. And when he finally shows his despair with a deep guttural roar, we're filled with more than a ton of jitters.

We owe most of our horrific pleasure to the actor Boris **Karloff** and his **makeup** artist, Jack B. Pierce. In the movie *Frankenstein,* made in 1931, these two men established the standard for future interpretations of the story. Since then, when one hears the name Frankenstein, one thinks of Boris Karloff's monster.

It took quite some effort to turn Boris into a convincing monster. He had to sit through 3½ hours of makeup work each time he appeared before the camera. His gear weighed more than 50 pounds, including the metal splints in his pant legs, which gave him his famous stiff walk.

The film was a hit at the box office and is now an absolute classic. Many other versions of the story have appeared since—some of them are dull versions of the original, others are classic themselves.

Frankenstein fanatics will want to see them all. There's *Son of Frankenstein* (1939), *The Ghost of Frankenstein* (1942), *Frankenstein Meets the Wolf Man* (1943), *House of Frankenstein* (1944), *The Curse of Frankenstein* (1957), *I Was a Teenage Frankenstein* (1957), *Abbott and Costello Meet Frankenstein* (1948), *Frankenstein Must Be Destroyed!* (1970), *The Revenge of Frankenstein* (1958), *Frankenstein Conquers the World* (1966), *Frankenstein 1970* (1958), and *Frankenstein Created Woman* (1967).

One of the many films deserves a special mention: *The Bride of Frankenstein* (1935), which is so funny that it hurts.

It's not only the original Frankenstein film that is a classic, but also the following "knock knock" joke:

FULL MOON

In the November issue of the *Monday Messenger,* a monthly magazine for **vampires, werewolves,** and other monsters fond of traveling, the following article appeared:

HIT OF THE SEASON:
COSTA DE LA LUNA

An ice-cold tip for all moon-starved monsters who like to freeze at leisure in the moonlight: the Costa de la Luna!

This moonlit coast, bathed by the grubby and muddy waves of the contaminated swampy ocean, offers the ideal opportunity to deepen your moon pallor. Impress friends at home with your wonderfully ashen complexion!*

Luxuriate on pleasantly gulchy bays where storms roar reassuringly. Stroll down the moony meadows of nettles, poison ivy fields, and mistletoe orchards. Enjoy refreshing moon-ripened fruit drinks on the idyllic moon terrace at the hotel ruins.

Yes, there is no doubt about it! An unforgettable vacation awaits you on the Costa de la Luna, land of the eternal full moon!

* CAUTION: Don't forget to protect yourself from a painful moonburn! Moonglasses, a moonhat, a beach paraluna, and moon lotion with moon protection factor (MPF) 15 are recommended.

FUNNY MONSTERS

Monsters are supposed to scare us. They make our teeth chatter and give us **goose bumps.** They are not meant to make us laugh. But some monsters thumb their noses at this idea and do exactly that. Here are a few famous funny monsters:

Kurt Halbritter has created a whole collection of unusual monsters in his book *Halbritter's Animal and Plant World.*

Maurice Sendak wrote and illustrated a classic monster story for children: *Where the Wild Things Are.*

Edward Koren's hairy monsters behave like completely normal humans. You'll choke with laughter when you recognize yourself and the monster in you.

Gahan Wilson's jokes are so macabre that you won't know whether to laugh or faint.

Dr. Seuss (Theodor Geisel) drew monsters for children and gave advice about how to keep these extravagant creatures as pets.

CONTINUED ON P. 61

G

"Made in Japan"
—INSCRIPTION FOUND ON A MOUND OF
UNIDENTIFIED OBJECTS IN THE YEAR 3025

GODZILLA

It's no coincidence that the making of the Japanese film *Godzilla, King of the Monsters* (1954) followed U.S. atom-bomb testing in the Pacific Ocean. It didn't help much, as far as the testing was concerned—but it did do a  lot for a few people's bank accounts.

The story can be quickly told: Disturbed during its afternoon nap by an atom-bomb explosion, the 900-foot-tall dinosaurlike monster surfaces from the depths of the ocean. It tramples half of Tokyo, gobbles up train cars, and shoves ocean liners around as if they were rubber ducks in a bathtub. Roaring defiantly, it blasts radioactive flares wildly in all directions. When this giant is fired at by heavy artillery, it doesn't even bat an eyelash. But fear not—after two hours of pulse-throbbing suspense, the movie comes to an end, as does the King of Monsters. (Who should actually be called "Queen," because Japanese **dragons** are female.)

For this movie, the filmmakers decided not to build a giant model of Godzilla. Instead, they built a miniaturized Tokyo, the size of a toy model. The filmmakers evidently determined that it was cheaper to crush toy houses than real ones. The visual effect was (nearly) the same in the end, however.

The success of the film was so great that Godzilla was revived in 1959 with *Gigantis, the Fire Monster.* Not far behind were *Godzilla versus the Thing* (1964); *Son of Godzilla* (1967); and *King Kong versus Godzilla* (1963). (There are two versions of the **King Kong** film. In the U.S. version, King Kong is victorious; in the Japanese version, Godzilla wins.)

The Japanese movie industry then decided to bring other, smaller living creatures into focus and enlarge them gigantically. Humanity was thus threatened by a moth (*Mothra,* 1962), a lizard (*Gorath,* 1962), a jellyfish (*Dogora: The Space Monster,* 1964), a snapping turtle (*The Invincible Gammera,* 1964), a crab (*Ebirah: Terror of the Deep,* 1966), a winged fox (*Gyaos,* 1967), and an extraterrestrial octopus (*Viras,* 1967).

So far, we have survived these onslaughts with little damage. And there definitely are other small animals that have caused us more trouble in their original size: fleas, lice, mosquitoes....

COMMON
FLEA

GOLEM

You can make a golem yourself: Take a lump of clay and shape it into a small figure. Write the word *emet* (Hebrew for *truth*) on its forehead. Then search for the right magic formula in the cabala (a particular medieval interpretation of the Jewish scriptures). Recite the formula over the clay figure. Of course, you must do this during a full moon, when toads are croaking their loudest.

Did you try it? And nothing happened? I bet you forgot to sprinkle the figure with the juice of an amanita (a poisonous mushroom)!

Okay, try again. And *still* nothing happened? Did you remember that it has to be a Friday the Thirteenth? Hmmmm...

Now don't get all frazzled. Check your calendar and make sure you have the right ingredients. Ready? Begin!

Finally, the small clay figure begins to grow. It rapidly becomes bigger, until at last a gigantic clay colossus stands before you. It asks you what your heart desires.

From now on, it takes out the trash for you, washes the dishes, cleans your room, and gives those bullies down the block a thorough scare. Unfortunately, you still have to do your homework yourself. The golem is a bit behind the times and doesn't know a thing about French or Spanish vocabulary or calculating percentages.

Before you go to bed, erase the first *e* on the golem's forehead, leaving only the word *met* (Hebrew for *dead*). Then the monster will shrink back to the size of the small clay figure and you can store it on your nightstand.

This whole procedure can be somewhat dangerous, however. Centuries ago in the village of Prague, Rabbi Loew created a golem to protect his people from attacks by Christians. One evening he forgot to erase the *e*, and the golem went berserk.

Luckily, it all ended well—otherwise the world would no longer exist. Yet the monster is merely sleeping, lying in some corner, dusty and unnoticed. No one knows where. And no one knows who will call it back to life. And no one knows when....

All we know for certain is:

1. In Hebrew, *golem* means shapeless mass; a Jewish figure of legend, a supernatural being who was given life by humans. It is a forerunner of **Frankenstein** and **mechanical monsters.**

2. *Der Golem* (1914), a novel by Gustav Meyrink.

3. *Der Golem* (1915), a film by Paul Wegener. (Except for a few feet of film, the whereabouts of this classic are unknown.)

4. *Der Golem and die Tanzerin (The Golem and the Dancer)* (1917), a film by Paul Wegener.

5. *Der Golem, wie er in die Welt kam (The Birth of the Golem)* (1920). Director: Paul Wegener; the golem: Paul Wegener; script: Paul Wegener.

GOOSE BUMPS

When Count **Dracula** chomps into a juicy neck, a **werewolf** ferociously bares its teeth, or the **Phantom of the Opera** scurries along dark and grim corridors, we get goose bumps—it's unavoidable. Our skin looks like that of a plucked goose.

And where do these strange bumps come from? Almost all over our bodies, we have tiny hairs. Beneath the skin, each individual hair is attached to a tiny muscle. When these mini-muscles contract, they produce little bumps around the hairs and make the hairs stand on end.

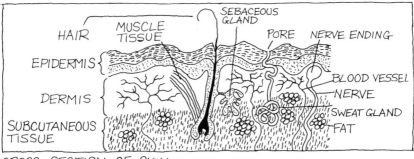

CROSS—SECTION OF SKIN

Why do we have such a ridiculous reaction to horror and terror? Take a dog or a cat, for example. When these animals smell danger or feel threatened, the fur on their necks, shoulders, backs, and tails bristles. As a true Monster Fan, you will certainly have noticed that fear—even on the hottest of summer days—is accompanied by a sensation of coldness. Raised hairs protect the body from the cold and keep muscles warm for the expected battle. And the psychological effect on the opponent is not to be underestimated: bushy hair or fur makes one look bigger and more terrifying.

Ages and ages ago, when we were still allowed to call our gorilla neighbors Uncle and Aunt, this ability of ours may indeed have impressed our enemies. We had hairier bodies in those days.

Nowadays, our goose bumps wouldn't impress a single vampire or werewolf. Not that we have much need to do so, anyway.

Nevertheless, friends of horror, these goose bumps are to be enjoyed—as a reminder of our **King-Kong**-like past!

GRIFFINS

You've never seen a griffin? These beasts have the head, breast, wings, and forelegs of an eagle, and the body, hindquarters, and tail of a lion. They guard fabulous treasures. If you want to find one, set off to the land of the Northwind people in Mongolia, or to the Arimaspians, the one-eyed Scythians. Since griffins eat horses, use a bike to get there. But be careful! Griffins nourish their offspring on humans!

Griffins are enormous—so enormous that you could use one of their claws for a wine barrel. In fact, their claws change color when they come into contact with certain poisons. Despite the dangers, tracking a griffin can be worthwhile: their nests are made of pure gold and their eggs are precious stones.

Griffins are ancient. A 5,000-year-old drawing of one of these creatures was found in the ancient city of Susa, Persia (in present-day Iran). Nowadays, many griffins are forced to earn their daily meat by ornamenting coats of arms.

H

"Trick or treat!"
—A GRAND AMERICAN TRADITION

HALLOWEEN

All Saints' Day and All Souls' Day are rather grim holidays in most European countries. It's a time to pay your respects to the dead, so people visit cemeteries. Because it's November, the weather is usually lousy, foggy, and cold. The highlight of the day is often not more than a handful of roasted chestnuts and the relief of getting out of the cold on arriving home.

The United States has its own celebration of the dead, but it's quite another thing. Halloween is the festival of monsters and ghosts. Scarecrows dangle from bare treetops. Jack-o'-lanterns perch comfortably on doorsteps. Devils, witches, **vampires,** skeletons, **mummies,** and **zombies** scurry past in the dusk.

Yes, it's a heyday for Monster Fans. You put on your costume and mask and are for once allowed to terrify the whole neighborhood. You pound on doors and scream threateningly, "Trick or treat!" A treat, as you know, can be anything from hot chocolate to candy or money, given to you by "terrified" adults to appease your awful temper. If someone doesn't have a treat handy, a trick is sure to follow. You and the rest of your spooky mob seek revenge.

It's a nice custom, don't you think? Halloween is an important celebration, because it reminds us of the possibility of the supernatural—adding a few spine-chilling thrills to our otherwise ordinary and rather humdrum lives.

HULK

"Hulk angry!" screams the green-skinned creature with the bulging biceps and shredded purple pants. "Hulk smash!" He lifts his hefty fist and swings hard—

The California coast between San Francisco and Los Angeles lies in ruins. Insulted and pouting, Hulk stomps off. But no matter where he goes, he can't find peace. The U.S. Army is constantly on his heels. Yet Hulk is invincible. The only thing that can cause him pain is to be called a monster.

The invention of comic book creators Stan Lee and Jack Kirby, Hulk has distinguished himself from the masses of run-of-the-mill **comic book monsters.** He has surpassed many courageous superheroes in popularity.

Why is this destructive, ugly monster so popular? Maybe it's because Hulk is not always Hulk. He is normally a human being named Bruce Banner, an atomic scientist who loves his country and humanity.

Bruce Banner is working dedicatedly on an experiment for the government—a gamma bomb—when there is an accident. He is exposed to a dangerous dose of gamma rays, and before you can say "Jack Robinson," he turns into the Hulk. Hulk doesn't know that he is also Bruce Banner. Just the same, when Hulk is blasted with gamma rays, he turns back into Bruce Banner. And when sensitive Bruce is under stress or in a frustrating situation—presto—he's Hulk again. Because of their difference in size, each transformation tears another new suit to shreds.

The idea that a violent monster dwells inside such an upright citizen could be the key to this comic's success. After a bad day—when everything has gone wrong and the whole world has dumped its problems and frustrations on you—who wouldn't like to turn into Hulk? To be able to dish it out for once, to be able to smash everything to pieces....

Monster Fans, beware! There's a Hulk in each and every one of us!

HULLABUB BASH

(Hullabaloo + Hubbub = Hullabub)

If you think that monsters can do whatever they like, then you're wrong. In social situations, they have to behave according to strict rules of etiquette.

Just as we are taught to nicely greet our aunt or grandmother—with a gentle kiss on the cheek, and an inquiry about her health—monsters with manners must pluck a few hairs from their aunts' chins, while grossly burping their greetings. It's only a question of decency!

ILLUS. 1a   ILLUS. 1b

The following text has been taken from the work *Proper Behavior for a Young Monster of Good Family* and describes the ceremony to be observed in giving a hullabub bash. Before you read on, however, you must swear on **Dracula**'s teeth not to use the following, absolutely confidential information—meant only for monsters—at your next party.

Guidelines for Giving a Gigantic
HULLABUB BASH

For the proper celebration of this social occasion, it is of utmost importance to have an orderly, clean, and elegant apartment or house at your disposal. Furthermore, care should be taken to

ILLUS. 2

DANCE COURSE

WITH MONSTER STOMP-STEP

The Tango

RIGHT 1-2-3!

LEFT 1-2-3!

TURN!

STOMP!

STOMP!

ROAR!

JUMP!

LAND!

BOW LOW!

invite at least 30 full-blooded monsters from families of high social standing.

After greeting the guests ceremoniously (see ILLUS. 1b), have your guests register in the guest book. Ask each new arrival to dunk its hand in the mustard or ketchup container set up for this purpose, then slap its "signature" on a white surface, preferably a wall or tablecloth.

It's then time for the quite popular and entertaining game, "High-Flying Fracas." Each guest tries to cross the room without touching the floor. The athletic monster, for example, leaps gracefully from cupboard to coatrack, swings from curtain rod to sofa, and with the aid of a crystal chandelier, clambers to the top of the potted palm. The one who smashes the most porcelain in the process is the winner.

The highlight of every hullabub bash is unquestionably the "Bloodbath Melee." Rare red wines are poured into balloons, which are then tightly knotted. Each guest is given an ample number of these balloon-bombs. At their pleasure, the participants may pelt each other with these projectiles, which explode on contact in such a manner as to resemble blood. When a guest has been hit, it is in good form for the guest to act as if he or she were dying. The victors are those who have not been "killed."

Certain social conventions should be minded in preparing and consuming a hullabub dinner. Everything edible in the fridge and pantry is diced and put in the mixer. Not only should eggs, pickles, chocolate, sardines, baloney, and candy bars be added, but also a squirt of toothpaste and a pinch of salt. Place this gooey mixture in a pot and heat it over the low flame of a bonfire built on a Persian carpet, until the sauce is sticky and doughy. Each guest is allowed to form his or her own head-sized ball of dough. The guests then throw these wads upward with both force and skill, so that they remain stuck to the ceiling. They then position themselves under the wads, open their mouths and wait* until the balls become unstuck and fall. May your guests' patience be rewarded with the most scrumptious of savory delights.

---

*In keeping with the best of table manners, the guests burp and drool while they wait.

No traditional hullabub is complete without music and dance. If an orchestra cannot be hired, it is permissible to place a few Beethoven LPs on hot plates until they ripple nicely. Then put them on the record player, hold the needle down firmly, and allow the ripples to sway you!

To end the party on a pleasant note, stage a reading from the host's collection of love letters. Good breeding, however, demands that this be done over loudspeakers, which allows the neighbors to join in the fun.

A hullabub celebrated in this fashion is in complete correspondence to the rules of etiquette and will surely be a smashing success.

I

"   !"

—INVISIBLE PROVERB

INVISIBLE MAN

The sensitive Monster Fan knows what it's like to lie in wait for something terrifying to appear: It's dark...you hear strange sounds—or at least you think you do....Yes, now you hear the sound of footsteps in the distance. Then silence. A door creaks. A draft as cold as the grave grazes your cheek. You anticipate something awful. A faint light comes nearer. It vanishes. Stillness. You wait again...then you hear a tap, tap, tap....

You hold your breath. Your heart is pounding wildly. You feel **goose bumps** on the back of your neck. You don't think you can hold out much longer. And then—finally—the monster appears. No matter how dangerous it looks or how terribly it roars, it is almost a relief after the unbearable tension of waiting. Now, at least, the horror has a name.

There's a story by H. G. Wells that makes use of this type of suspense: *The Invisible Man*. No one actually sees this monster. They only hear its footsteps and see its tracks in the snow.

Sometimes someone will see a lit cigarette hovering above an armchair. In company, it dresses up in high-necked clothing, gloves, and dark glasses. With bandages wrapped around its head, no one can tell that there is absolutely nothing underneath.

And now, *Monster Manual* shall unveil the secret of the Invisible Man: the monster is really Jack Griffin, a mad scientist. While experimenting with the drug monocaine and using himself as a guinea pig, Griffin suddenly becomes invisible. Unnoticed, he commits the most awful crimes. He is aware of the advantages of being invisible and wants to take over the world. The question is, is he aware of the drawbacks?

The Invisible Man was made into a movie in 1933. It was followed by a number of other invisible-creature capers, including *The Invisible Man Returns* (1940) and *The Invisible Woman* (1941).

GLORP BARES HIS TEETH AND DROOLS HUNGRILY.

YOU HAVE A CAVITY--FIRST MOLAR, BOTTOM LEFT. YOU SHOULD GO TO THE DENTIST!

CONTINUED ON P. 68

J

"How cheerfully he seems to grin,
How neatly spreads his claws,
And welcomes little fishes in,
With gently smiling jaws!"
—LEWIS CARROLL

JAWS

Jaws is the title of one of Steven Spielberg's earliest and most horrifying films.

A huge white shark mingles with the sea-bathing guests of a summer resort. Every now and then it nibbles at a few toes or feet that swim by. Sometimes, it even chomps off a bit more: a whole leg or even a whole tourist. It's terrible for the tourist trade, and for that reason, the whole affair is hushed up. The hungry shark is able to enjoy a few more snacks. Finally, a famous shark hunter, the town's sheriff, and a marine biologist all team up to hunt the killer shark.

Of course, sharks aren't all really as vicious and bloodthirsty as the monster in this movie. Yet sharks continue to be slaughtered—partly because of human fear.

Here's a little food for thought: Is it a coincidence that certain bats (see: **vampires**), wolves (see: **werewolves**), and apes (see: **King Kong**) are among the world's endangered species?

JEKYLL AND HYDE

The Scottish writer Robert Louis Stevenson (1850–1894) specialized in writing charming essays, poetry, and travel books. But he is probably best remembered for his adventure stories, *Treasure Island* and *Kidnapped*, and for the terrifying tale of horror called *The Strange Case of Dr. Jekyll and Mr. Hyde*.

Dr. Jekyll is a highly respected, honorable scientist. Passionately, he works away in his lab. One night, while mixing and concocting, he happens to invent a mysterious potion. He takes a sip. His body jerks in agonizing pain and begins to change.

When the pain subsides, Jekyll has transformed into a new being—Mr. Hyde. He is smaller, younger, apelike, and indescribably evil. Mr. Hyde now sets off into the dark night of London to indulge in his vices and to commit the most awful of crimes. When he is in danger of being caught, he rushes back to the lab. He takes another sip of the potion, and Dr. Jekyll, the man of good name, replaces the monster.

What all started as a scientific experiment becomes an addiction. Jekyll struggles desperately to resist, but the monster in him forces him to hit the bottle more and more often.

It is an odd coincidence that Stevenson's death has a great resemblance to a scene in *Dr. Jekyll and Mr. Hyde*. On December 3, 1894, the 44-year-old Stevenson opened a bottle of wine. Suddenly, he cringed and screamed in fright: "What's happening to me? Has my face changed?" He collapsed and died from a stroke.

The horrific Mr. Hyde has become a favorite monster of movie directors. By 1920 there were 10 silent movies based on this story. In 1931 actor Fredric March was awarded an Oscar for his portrayal of Mr. Hyde. Yes, Mr. Hyde—so far the only monster to have won an Academy Award.

K

"There's no business like show business."
—AN UNQUESTIONABLY TRUTHFUL STATEMENT

KARLOFF, BORIS

Perhaps no one besides his mother and his **makeup** artist knew what Boris Karloff (1887–1969) really looked like. He faced the rest of the world behind masks of horror.

Karloff was discovered and became famous almost overnight through the movie *Frankenstein,* in 1931. What accounted for the immense fame of this rather slight and modest man? *Frankenstein* director James Whale believed it had to do with Karloff's eyes. They had a hungry look about them, even when Karloff had just finished eating.

After *Frankenstein,* Karloff went on to play dozens of other great monster roles. He must have spent half his time in the makeup chair, where he was transformed into the monster of the day, and the rest of his time in front of the camera, waving his arms like a madman. This evidently kept him fit. Boris Karloff lived to the age of 82.

THREE FACES OF BORIS KARLOFF:

KING KONG

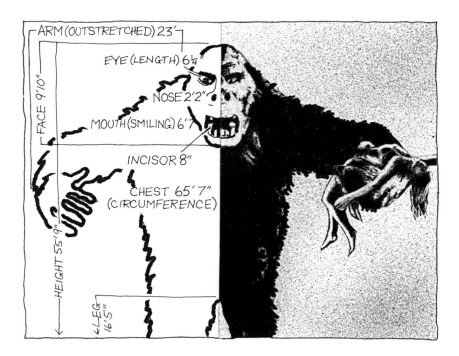

On the top of the Empire State Building, an incredible scene unfolds. An enormous ape holds a young woman clenched in his huge paw. Airplanes swarm around his head, and he swats at them like flies. Machine-gun volleys are a mere annoyance. When the ape pounds its chest victoriously, the mighty skyscraper shakes. Yet the monster is devastated, crushed: it loves the woman in its paw, but she does not return his affection. Carefully, he places the unconscious woman on a ledge, sadly roars one last time, totters, and falls to the streets below. King Kong does not survive.

When *King Kong* was released in 1933, it was the biggest box-office hit the movie industry had seen. The film premiered in the two largest movie houses in New York, which together accommodated 10,000 viewers. The movie houses were packed for every showing, 10 times a day.

No expenses or pains had been spared in producing the film. The famous mystery writer Edgar Wallace was flown in from England and wrote the script, with a few others, in eight weeks. When the monster himself, King Kong, was designed, a team of builders created 27 different large models of the beast. The largest model was more than 52 feet tall. The love scene between King Kong and his sweetheart, Fay Wray, lasted a mere 30 seconds on-screen but took 23 hours to shoot.

Unfortunately, Edgar Wallace did not live to see the movie's premiere. He died exactly a year before the film opened.

"Darn it all, where is the exiiiiiiii...???!!!"
—LAST WORDS OF A LABYRINTH VISITOR

LABYRINTH

You're cautiously groping down a narrow, dark passageway. Moss and slimy lichen cover the walls. You creep along with your head bent down, because the ceiling is low and damp, and cobwebs brush against your hair. Now and again, a cold drop of water slides down the back of your neck. You step on something soft and slippery—it moves and tries to crawl up your leg. Repulsed, you shake the thing off and quickly stumble on. Behind you, a rat darts by. In front of you, you hear the flapping of bat wings. Suddenly, you reach a fork in the path and you decide, hesitantly, to take the passage to the right. It winds along, downward, upward, to the left, to the right—and again to the left and again to the right. At an oddly shaped stone, you realize in a panic that you passed this spot once before—hours ago. Or was it days ago? You continue on. Again and again, the path twists and turns. There are crossings, side passageways, recesses, and chambers. Corridor after

corridor goes nowhere, ending at a wall or dropping off into darkness. You anxiously wonder how long your weakly glowing flashlight will hold out. With each decision you make, you are tortured by uncertainty, not knowing whether you've made the choice that will lead you out of the darkness and into the light of day.

All right, you may breathe more freely now—you've woken from your nightmare in the labyrinth. Labyrinths are pure torture for humans, but an absolute paradise for monsters. They are their favorite kind of place. The famous Minotaur (see: **monsters of Greek mythology**) is only one of many monsters who enjoyed such a residence.

The labyrinth illustrated on page 67 will give you a faint notion of the horror of a true labyrinth. If you look at the whole picture from above, however, it isn't too difficult to find the exit. For added suspense, try this trick: Cut a hole, about ½-inch wide, in the middle of a piece of paper. Place this peephole over the young damsel-in-distress in the labyrinth's center. Now slide this hole along the passageways and try to find the exit. If you run into a monster, turn back. Take a deep breath and begin again.

GLORP ROARS THE ROAR THAT HAS MADE HUMAN BLOOD CURDLE SINCE THE BEGINNING OF TIME. (CONTINUED ON P. 74)

LOCH NESS

Shortly before the deadline for this book, a sensational headline hit the papers: "Loch Ness Monster Sighted Again!" Our foreign correspondent took the next plane to the site of the monster's appearance. Here is her report:

Dampness and fog cover the Scottish Highlands. When the taxi drops me off at Drumnadrochit, a small village on the shore of Loch Ness, I cannot see the lake. I can only see the backs of tourists crowding the shore. Their camcorders, cameras, and binoculars are aimed toward the lake, waiting for Nessie to appear. Nessie chooses not to. "She's kind of shy, you know," I'm told by the shopkeeper who sells me a booklet about Nessie.

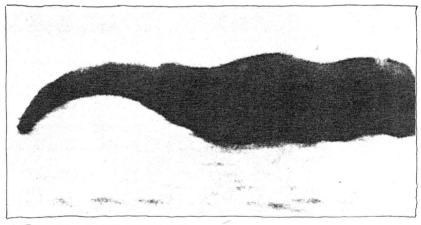

A PORTRAIT OF NESSIE?

The booklet tells me that *loch* is the Gaelic word for lake. Loch Ness is about 1 mile wide, 21 miles long, and more than 900 feet deep. The water's surface temperature is 54° F. Deeper below, temperatures reach only 41° F. The monster was first sighted in A.D. 565, and since 1933, Nessie makes her appearance only once a year, usually in summer.

I hire a tour guide. McNepp, a typical Highlander, rents a boat and we float out onto the lake. No Nessie. "This time of day, she usually takes her nap. She gets tired with all this tourist business about, you know," McNepp explains, and he offers to sell me some picture postcards of Nessie.

Suddenly, not far from our boat, the surface of the water begins to bubble. More bubbles appear, then a large, black object rises from the depths and emerges in a turmoil of crashing waves. It's huge, threatening. It is not Nessie. It is a submarine.

"I know she's there," says McSearch, captain of the submarine. We are having lunch a while later at Nessie's Snack Attack in the village. Chewing on a piece of Nessie Monster Steak, he continues, "You know, Nessie is fond of playing hide-and-seek. But I'll get her, don't you worry!"

Passing shops with Nessie T-shirts, Nessie teacups, and Nessie ashtrays, I make my way back to the taxi stop. I cast a long last look upon the eerie lake. No sign of Nessie.

"Try again next summer," says the driver. "She'll be around as long as people enjoy deep dark secrets and are willing to pay for them." We speed off down the dirt road, leaving behind the un-solved mystery of Nessie, shrouded in the fog and the dark waters of the loch....

On the British Isles, people seem to be quite taken with monsters of the liquid element. Most of these creatures don't have names they can call their own; more likely, they are called "the monster of such-and-such lake." But water monsters have been known to rise for a gulp of fresh air from certain North American lakes as well. Many have names that come from Native American legends.

Here is a dry and unromantic list of a few of these creatures, who are grouped by their country of origin:

Name	Residence	Country	Discovered	Appearance
Nessie	*Loch Ness*	Scotland	A.D. 565	long neck, curved back, Plesiosaur-like
Monster of Loch Arkaig		Scotland	1857	horselike
Morgawr	*coast of Cornwall*	England	1975	black, dinosaur-like, green eyes
Monster of Lough Shanakever		Ireland	1955	donkeylike, black
Monster of Lough Auna		Ireland	end of 19th century	cross between a horse and an eel, humps
Monster of Lough Ree		Ireland	1960	long neck, flat head, hunchback
Monster of Lough Brin		Ireland	1979	cross between a seal and a dragon, black
Monster of Lough Nahooin		Ireland	1968	sea serpent, spines along back, stomach, and mouth, light in color
Caddy	*Strait of Georgia*	Canada	1932	snakelike
Ogopogo	*Lake Okanagan*	Canada	1850	snakelike, dark green
Igopogo	*Lake Simcoe*	Canada	1952	doglike head, neck like a stovepipe
Manipogo	*Lake Manitoba*	Canada	1908	black sea serpent, toots like a locomotive
Ponik	*Lake Pohenegamook*	Canada	1874	manatee-like, spiny black fin
Angeoa	*Iliamna Lake*	U.S. (Alaska)	end of 19th century	fishlike
Champ	*Lake Champlain*	U.S. (on NY–VT border)	1819	Plesiosaur-like

**M** "*You can tell a monster by the company he keeps.*"
—A TIP FOR ALL MONSTER FANS FROM YOURS TRULY

MAKEUP

You want to be a monster for **Halloween?** *Monster Manual* makes it possible! We sent our star reporter to a movie studio, where she received a few inside tips from the screen's top-notch makeup artists.

BEFORE YOU BEGIN:

 All materials referred to here are available at your local drugstore. Larger cities have stores that sell **theater** supplies.

 Before applying makeup, wash your face with mild soap, and moisturize with an oil-free lotion.

 Keep makeup utensils (brushes, puffs, etc.) clean, so that the colors stay fresh and bright.

 Take your time. For the mask shown here, you'll need about an hour.

 To remove makeup, use a special makeup-removal cream. Then wash your face with mild soap and warm water.

  To transform yourself into a **vampire,** you'll need: white greasepaint (clown white), blue and red makeup sticks, red lipstick, black eyebrow pencil, a small sponge, artificial blood, plastic fangs, and a wig.

1. With your fingers, dab a foundation layer of white greasepaint all over your face and neck. Use a damp sponge to spread it evenly.

2. With the blue makeup stick, draw a thick line on both sides of your face, just below your cheekbones. Spread it downward a bit with your fingertips. Do the same with the red makeup, so that the colors blend into a nice purplish hue.

3. Draw a thick blue line above your eyes. Using your fingers, smudge the color over your eyelids and out toward your temples. Repeat this process with red makeup, blending the colors together.

4. With the red makeup stick, draw a sweeping line along the upper edge of the purple area, just below your eyebrows. It should end at the temples. Put on lipstick. Apply red and blue makeup under your eyes, as in step 3.

5. With the black eyebrow pencil, darken eyebrows. They should taper outward into fine lines. Pencil thick black lines along the bottom of your eyelids and under your eyes.

6. Dip the tips of the plastic fangs in artificial blood. Paint a few drops of blood at the corner of your mouth. Put on a black wig. Now snicker hideously.

Since your imagination knows no limits, the above example should inspire you to create new disguises. You've got the basic know-how. Now it's just a question of trial and error. But don't forget: Practice makes the perfect monster!

CONTINUED ON P. 78

MANTICORE

Legend tells us that the manticore was an animal having the head of a man—often with horns—the body of a lion, and the tail of a dragon or scorpion. Although its actual existence seems unlikely, this mysterious monster can be found in a zoology book from 1658! The book describes it as follows: It lives in India, grows to the size of a horse, and feeds exclusively on human flesh. The manticore is a kind of anthropophagus—a people-eating creature. The book's author did not seem to doubt the manticore's existence. He claims that his account is based on reports from sailors, world travelers, and scientists.

Our biology books no longer include the manticore. Too bad. It certainly sounds more interesting than the usual dull reports on the common leech (*Fasciola hepatica*) from the class of annelid worms (Hirudinea).

MECHANICAL MONSTERS

ROBOT   ANDROID   CYBORG

Let's get it straight. There are:

ROBOTS (from Czech: *robota* = work) are machines created to relieve people of work they don't want to do, can't do, or are plain too lazy to do. In books and movies, they look like tin cans with arms and legs, or like electronically operated knights in armor. But less human-looking robots actually exist, and they are used worldwide in business and industry.

COMPUTERS (from Latin: *com* = with, *putare* = to think) are the intellectuals of the mechanical world. Unlike robots, they are not mobile. But they run whole factories, steer spaceships, and rule humanity (this last—so far—only in science fiction).

ANDROIDS (from Greek: *andros* = man, *oid* = similar) are robots (strictly fictional) that have been given a human appearance. They are employed as agents, police officers, or killers.

CYBORGS (from English: CYBernetic ORGanism) are technically humans, but they have little they can call their own, aside from their brains. They are neatly packaged and put into the body of a robot or an android. Such brains can then be sent on journeys

or missions for which a human body would be too weak and a mechanical brain too inflexible.

In science fiction, mechanical monsters can be either good or bad. Good ones usually accompany space explorers on their excursions. Unlike human heroes, who are usually extremely serious, robots, androids, and cyborgs are clowns and provide comic relief from the high-tension suspense. For example, there is Robby the Robot (*Forbidden Planet,* 1956), Twiki (*Buck Rogers in the 25th Century,* 1979), or C-3PO and R2D2 (*Star Wars,* 1977), who some people have called the Laurel and Hardy of the robot world.

The bad ones—those oversized tin cans with the little red lightbulbs for eyes—have all been programmed for the same screenplay. The story can be told quickly:

Scientist (mad) builds robot (big, strong, invincible). Robot has ability to emit deadly X rays from left nostril. Scientist loses control over mechanical monster. Robot kills scientist and steals beautiful woman. Woman dangles helplessly in steel claws of robot. Woman screeches **"eeeeeeeeeek,"** and in R-rated version is scantily dressed. Army, Air Force, and Marines are called to action. Male hero finishes monster off with a knitting needle. Woman intact. World badly damaged. The End.

To be honest—who hasn't been frustrated by modern technology?

GLORP BECOMES VERY, VERY SAD.

(CONTINUED ON P. 89)

MINI-MONSTERS

More than 20 years ago, a creative group of people decided to put children's obsession with television to good use. The question was, how would they get children to watch one certain program? Right—with monsters!

Jim Henson (1936–1990), the creator of the Muppets, designed a bunch of lovable, laughable monsters. Then he wrote some funny dialogue, hired a team of people to work with him, and the show was on its way. The first episode of *Sesame Street* was shown in 1969 to a large and varied audience. Infants, toddlers, schoolkids, college students, mothers, fathers, grandmas, and grandpas all sat glued to the screen when it was time for *Sesame Street*. Everyone, young and old, learned their ABCs.

The *Sesame Street* monsters aren't scary. They each have their own special personality, quirks, and shortcomings. That's what makes them so likable. They are just plain monsters, like you and me.

Here's a list of a few of these mini-monster stars:

THE COUNT: To Monster Fans, his resemblance to **Dracula** actor Bela Lugosi is striking. Truly obsessed, he counts anything and everything. Bats, rats, the lids of coffins...nothing is safe from his counting-mania. It goes without saying that the Count is responsible for the show's mathematical lessons.

COOKIE MONSTER: He's always hungry, especially for cookies. Occasionally he will gulp down old shoes, cellos, and windowpanes. In his deep rumbling voice he will tell you, "When me hungry, me also eat car tires. But cookies better!"

OSCAR THE GROUCH: A decided misanthrope (someone who hates or distrusts humanity). He lives alone in a dented trash can. He is an absolute grump. A friendly word is enough to set off his temper. He loves old junk, rotten rubbish, and anything ugly.

BERT: A thorough pessimist, and with reason. He is a victim of the most incredible mishaps. But he takes each blow calmly. As he puts it, "I knew all along things would go wrong."

ERNIE: Bert's pal and a true optimist. He usually strolls through town in a great mood. When a flowerpot falls from a 27th-story window and lands three feet away from him, he chuckles in delight. His favorite thing is his rubber ducky.

GROVER: The youngest of the group. He's childish, cute, and clumsy. He has a quite unusual wish for a monster—he wants to be big and strong.

Who's who?
As an attentive reader (and most likely a one-time *Sesame Street* fan), can you name the Muppets in the picture above? (See: Solutions on p. 140.)

MONSTERS OF GREEK MYTHOLOGY

The horror caused by these monsters is merely moderate, and you won't get any **goose bumps** from them. Mythological monsters are a bit old and stale. Nevertheless, the inquiring Monster Fan would do well to make their acquaintance. Many contemporary monsters have their origins in Greek legends and myths.

The Greek gods were passionate lovers who had many affairs on the side. Their heavenly partners didn't like this one bit. As a result, the children from the secret romances were often turned into monsters, of a sort, by these ultrajealous husbands or wives. They became divine monsters, having special powers and specific realms of responsibility. They were said to be invincible. Yet, as legend has it, a hero usually turned up to do them in.

Here are some of the most important of these unearthly creatures, ranked not by their godliness, but in simple alphabetical order:

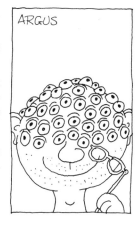

ARGUS was the famous 100-eyed guardian. He was created by the heavenly mother, HERA, to protect beautiful IO from the amorous advances of Hera's own husband, ZEUS. It was difficult to get anything past Argus's 100 eyes, yet HERMES—messenger of the gods—successfully caught Argus off guard and beheaded him.

Hera is said to have put Argus's eyes on the tail of the peacock. The expression "Argus-eyed" means highly observant and alert.

CHIRON
(CENTAUR)

CENTAURS, creatures that were half-horse and half-man, grazed in the plains of Thessaly. Evil centaurs were slain by the Greek god HERACLES (known to the Romans as HERCULES). Good centaurs became the instructors of heroes. CHIRON, a particularly wise and well-behaved centaur, was even promoted to the position of personal physician and tutor of the gods. (The word *chiro*practor has its roots in *Chiron.*)

CERBERUS, a three-headed, serpent-tailed watchdog, was posted at the entrance to Hades (the mythological underworld). He allowed no living creature to enter Hades and no deathly spirit to exit. Only three mortals were able to successfully overcome Cerberus: ORPHEUS, who charmed Cerberus with music; AENEAS, who fed him drugged food to make him sleep; and HERACLES, who used his strength.

CERBERUS

A guard, desk clerk, or receptionist who makes the entrance of a visitor extremely difficult is sometimes jokingly called "Cerberus."

CHIMERA is the part lion, part goat, fire-spitting serpent-tailed sister of CERBERUS. She was killed by the brave BELLEROPHON with the aid of his winged horse, PEGASUS. Nowadays, a chimera is a figment of the imagination, an illusion.

CYCLOPS

CYCLOPS were any of a race of giants who were said to have descended from the TITANS. They were known for their huge proportions and for having only one eye, located in the middle of their forehead.

ODYSSEUS once made the unpleasant acquaintance of the cyclops POLYPHEMUS. Yet by blinding it, Odysseus was able to flee.

ECHIDNA, half-woman and half-serpent, gave birth to CERBERUS, ORTHOS, HYDRA, CHIMERA, and SPHINX. She was a devoted and loving mother, until the day she was killed by ARGUS.

The **EUMENIDES** were a trio of serpent-haired, whip-wielding sisters: ALECTO, TISIPHONE, and MEGAERA. They were said to pursue and punish evildoers. Like a guilty conscience, they were hard to quiet. In Roman mythology, the Eumenides were called the FURIES.

GIANTS all had the same ancestors, the TITANS, but they differed in the quality of their ugliness. Some had 50 heads, others had dragonlike tails. Some had 100 arms, others the bodies of serpents. Yet all of them were huge, strong, and dumb. When they rebelled against ZEUS, our hero HERACLES finished them off. Mountains are said to be the tombs of giants.

HARPIES were loathsome vultures with the faces of old hungry women. Even more repulsive than their looks was their stench. It was so awful, in fact, that it caused the king of Thracia to starve to death! Only the din of a brass band could drive the harpies away. A lyre (a stringed instrument of the harp family) was always handy in those days, but a *brass band?*

HYDRA

HYDRA was a serpent of Lake Lerna. No one knows exactly how many heads she had, but when one of them was cut off, two would grow back in its place. When her time came, it was HERACLES (who else?) who put her to rest. In modern times, hydrants have survived to remind us of this water monster.

MEDUSA (CANNOT BE SHOWN— SEE TEXT)

MEDUSA, STHENO, and **EURATE** were sisters called the GORGONS. Stheno and Eurate resembled winged elephants, and Medusa, once lovely, was so disfigured by the jealous goddess ATHENA that no one could bear the sight of her. Those who dared to take a peek turned to stone. PERSEUS chopped off Medusa's head without giving her a glance— by viewing her reflection in his shield.

MINOTAUR

The **MINOTAUR** lived in the king of Crete's subterranean **labyrinth.** With the head of a bull and the body of a man, it roared terrifyingly and dined on the flesh of young humans. It was THESEUS who finally killed the Minotaur, putting an end to its awful behavior.

The **SIRENS** were a pair of feathered, fishtailed sea nymphs who lured sailors to their island with their bewitching song. ODYSSEUS wanted to hear them, but he knew what he was doing when he ordered his men to chain him to the ship's mast and to plug their ears with wax. The song of the Sirens is said to be so irresistible that those who heard it were compelled to abandon their ship and swim toward the singers, only to die in the swirling currents.

Nowadays, sirens are alarming rather than bewitching.

SCYLLA began her days as a beautiful nymph, then was turned into a sea monster by CIRCE, a sorceress. Scylla became part woman, part fish, with five heads and the heads of dogs growing from her waist. She lived in a cave above the Strait of Messina, where she ate innocent sailors who came too close. Just opposite her cave was a deadly whirlpool called Charybdis. Sailors had to risk one hazard or the other, or try to navigate their ship between the two. In recent years, things have been pretty quiet in this region. But Scylla's name still comes up occasionally when someone is in a tricky spot between two evils. It's then said that the person is caught "between Scylla and Charybdis."

The **SPHINX** was another of monster-mother ECHIDNA's daughters. With the head of a woman, the body of a lion, a serpent's tail, and wings, the Sphinx was a monster indeed. The Sphinx sat perched on a rock outside the city of Thebes. Whenever a wanderer came by, the Sphinx posed a riddle. When the right answer did not follow, then—chomp! The unfortunate person disappeared between her jaws. OEDIPUS was the first, and the last, to answer her riddle. The Sphinx's despair was so great that she committed suicide by throwing herself from the rock.

Each of the monsters listed here has its own story. Your neighborhood library is sure to have more books that tell their tales.

MORGENSTERN, CHRISTIAN

Don't get me wrong: Christian Morgenstern (1871–1941) was not
a monster. He was a poet. He wrote gruesome, beautiful poems.
He liked to play around with macabre, bizarre ideas. He didn't
take mysterious matters dead seriously; although he makes our
flesh creep, he also makes us laugh.

In his collection of poetry *The Gallows Songs*, strange monsters
run riot in the stormy darkness of night. There are silver horses,
owlworms, turtletoads, moonsheep, Midnight Mice, and Hawken
Chicks. The canyon canine and the newmoondame howl. A
sulfurhyena dances with a werefox, a Nightrogue pairs with a
Sevenswine, while the Fingoor stares goggle-eyed from the ponds.

Here is a short sample of Morgenstern's work:

The Fingoor

The nightalp chicken chuckles,
the windhorn ganders toot;
the swarthy swain unbuckles
his flute.

A he-owl, dove like, turtles
to woo his owlish she;
a little Six Nix hurtles
along from tree to tree...

And spooks their spook are wreaking,
and crows are cawing "croak";
and from the ponds are peeking
the Fingoor and her folk.

("The Fingoor," in *Christian Morgenstern's Galgenlieder (Gallow Songs),* translated and edited by Max E. Knight. [Berkeley: University of California Press,
1963]. Copyright © 1963 Max E. Knight.)

MUMMIES

In Egypt a few thousand years ago, it was the custom to preserve a person's remains after his or her death, so that the person could enjoy the afterlife. The brain and most other internal organs were removed from the body, and the body was stuffed with rags to dry it, then with bags of salt and herbs. The corpse was also bathed in a sodium solution until the skin was dried and leathery. It was rubbed with ointments and oils, then wrapped in long strips of linen. This process is called embalmment or mummification. The corpse, prepared in such a manner, is called a mummy.

Mummies were placed in a series of nested coffins and laid in a tomb. For the rich, these tombs were pyramids or other large structures carved of stone. They were sealed tightly to protect the valuable objects placed inside with the mummy.

"So what?" the disappointed Monster Fan asks. "Where is the horror, where are the monsters?"

Patience, patience—they're coming up next! Step back, but don't trip over any electrical cords! Okay, then—ready? Lights! Camera! Action!

Scene 17, take 3: A study. In a dark corner, an open sarcophagus; inside it is a mummy. Nearby is a desk, lit by a candle. A scientist is seated at the desk, bent over a papyrus scroll.

With effort, he deciphers and translates the hieroglyphs: "This is...the Book...of Thoth...." Cut.

Scene 18, take 1: Semi-close-up, motionless mummy in sarcophagus. The voice of the scientist: "...in which the magic words...are written...with which Isis brought Osiris...back to life." A bandage slowly unwinds and falls from the mummy's head. "Amon-Ra...God of the Gods...dead is the gate...to new life." More layers of bandages unwind. Cut.

Scene 19, take 1: Close-up, mummy. The scientist's voice, hoarse and faltering: "We live...today...we shall...live...again!" More and more layers of bandages fall from the mummy's face. Withered flesh and closed eyes become visible. The eyes slowly open. They glare coldly, rigidly. Cut.

Scene 20, take 1: The scientist leans more closely into the scroll. He reads: "In a variety of forms...we...shall...reappear!!!" The mummy, draped with a few tattered bands of cloth, suddenly emerges and moves stiffly behind the unaware scientist. It grabs the scroll and shuffles slowly, bandages dragging behind it, into the darkness of the night. Cut.

Scene 21, take 1: The scientist, madness reflected in his bulging eyes, his body unnaturally contorted, holding on to the desk for dear life, giggles queerly: "It's...it's...going for a walk!!" He slumps over the desk and lies motionless. The candle goes out. Cut.

This is just the beginning—nearly all movies with mummy monsters get off to such a start. And nearly all of them end tragically for the 3,700-year-old packaged cadavers. They are inevitably sent back, special delivery, to the realm of the dead.

All great monster actors have tried their hand at a mummy role at least once in their careers: Boris **Karloff**, Christopher Lee (see: **Dracula**), Lon **Chaney**, Jr.

Which actor looked best wrapped in bandages is left to your own personal taste and sense of horror.

MUNSTERS

No, it's not a spelling mistake—it's Munsters with a *u*. *The Munsters* is an old television sitcom that your parents enjoyed watching. Maybe you've seen the reruns.

The Munsters live in a typical one-family house at 1313 Mockingbird Lane, and have typical worries, joys, and hopes. Not at all typical is the fact that the head of the family, Herman Munster, looks like **Frankenstein's** monster, and his wife, Lily, looks very much like a **vampire.** Lily's father, Grandpa, resembles Bela Lugosi's **Dracula,** and Herman and Lily's eight-year-old offspring, Eddie, shows good promise of becoming a **werewolf.** The black sheep of the family is the niece, Marilyn. According to our standards, she is quite pretty, which means that the rest of the Munsters find her quite pitiful. ("Poor dear," they say, "it's not her fault.")

The series was not, of course, meant to horrify, but to amuse. It entertained audiences in prime time for two years, from 1964 to 1966.

NOW DON'T BE SO TOUCHY. IF IT MAKES YOU HAPPY, I'LL PRETEND TO BE AFRAID.

SUPER!

GLORP SMILES AND BRUSHES AWAY HIS TEARS.

CONTINUED ON P. 95

N

"Vampirism is a fate worse than death."
—TRANSYLVANIAN SAYING

NOSFERATU

According to eastern European fairy tales, a nosferatu is an undead being, a **vampire.**

Nosferatu: A Symphony of Horror is a silent movie made in 1921 by Friedrich Wilhelm Murnau. It was based on **Dracula,** a novel by Bram Stoker. The story was changed a bit and the setting moved from England to Germany. Count Dracula became Graf Orlok. Max Schreck played the part. Monster experts say he was the best vampire to ever flit across the screen. Pale and wispy, with long fingernails and pointed incisors, he cast bizarre shadows over his listless victims.

Years later, Werner Herzog directed a film based on the same material: *Nosferatu the Vampyre* (1979). Herzog stuck pretty much to the original silent version, and Klaus Kinski made a fine bald-headed blood addict.

MAX SCHRECK

KLAUS KINSKI

O

OGRES

Ogres are those really horrible, people-eating figures in fairy tales. After a hard day's work uprooting trees, they stomp into their caves and bawl: "Fee, fi, fo, fum, I smell the blood of an Englishman!" They lick their chops and drool all over their double chins.

Tastes differ. For us Monster Fans, Juicy Magic Hand Punch hits the spot better. Serve this beverage to your party guests on a ghastly late-October evening. (See directions on the next page.)

Juicy Magic Hand Punch

1. Pour raspberry juice into a clean rubber or plastic glove.

2. Tie off the top with a string or rubber band.

3. Put the hand (no, not yours) in the freezer overnight.

4. Hold the frozen hand (you know which one) for a moment under hot water, so that the rubber glove is easy to remove.

5. Place the hand in a punch bowl and add fruit juice. *Red* fruit juice, of course.

Not only does this look cannibalistic, it keeps the punch cold. After slurping and drinking to your heart's content, lick those sweet and sticky fingers. (Yes, your own, too.)

P

"Sticks and stones won't break my bones, but words will always hurt me."
—A TYPICAL PROBLEM OF INSECURE MONSTERS

PHANTOM OF THE OPERA

Paris's opera house is said to be built over medieval torture chambers and damp, cold dungeons. In this endless **labyrinth** of passageways dwells the Phantom: a shy, eccentric man who hides his disfigured, hideous face behind a death mask. Every now and then, he risks leaving his dark realm to listen, completely enraptured, to the music being sung on the stage above. Music is his only love—aside from a lovely woman who sings in the choir.

A French writer named Gaston Leroux wrote the story of the Phantom more than 80 years ago. Hollywood released a version in 1925, with master monster mime Lon **Chaney** playing the Phantom. *The Phantom of the Opera* was a great success worldwide.

LON CHANEY AS THE PHANTOM

There have been several remakes of the movie, but, as is often the case, the newer versions are pale phantoms of the great original. Since 1988, the Phantom has haunted a Broadway musical.

Phantoms are illusory images, as in a daydream or fantasy. They vanish as quickly as they appear. People who see a phantom usually freeze on the spot, mouth agape, eyes glassy and bulging, and turn as white as a sheet. After about 10 minutes, their tense muscles begin to relax, they wipe the cold sweat from their foreheads, scratch their heads, and ask themselves if they've really seen something or whether they've been hallucinating, dreaming, or have had one drink too many.

Feeble souls tend to calm themselves afterward with a swig of something fortifying. Orange juice or milk is recommended.

POE, EDGAR ALLAN

Edgar Allan Poe (1809–1849) didn't invent monsters in the usual sense. Open one of Poe's books, and you won't find any ferocious creature baring its teeth or stampeding major cities with an earsplitting roar. Poe's horror is more subtle. Stealthily, it creeps its way into your heart, and before you know it, you are sitting on the edge of your seat. You are holding your breath and your pulse is throbbing. And for all that, nothing has really happened yet.

Or almost nothing. You have digested only a few bizarre details: a crack in the wall that grows continuously larger; a black one-eyed cat whose white spot on its chest begins to look like a gallows; a raven that pecks insistently at a window one night; a small oval picture that seems to have some mysterious power over people.... These small terrors take on such dimensions that they dwarf even the most gigantic of monsters.

You can enjoy Poe's horror stories with a good conscience, because they are considered great literature. But don't expect to sleep peacefully after reading one of his tales.

Naturally, the movie business has tried its hand at Poe. Here are some films, available on video, that you may want to see:

Murders in the Rue Morgue (1932), *The Black Cat* (1934), *The Raven* (1935), *House of Usher* (1960), *The Pit and the Pendulum* (1961), *The Premature Burial* (1962), *The Raven* (1963), *The Masque of the Red Death* (1964), and *Tomb of Ligeia* (1965).

THE GIRL JITTERS AND QUIVERS,

AND SCREAMS AT THE TOP OF HER LUNGS.

CONTINUED ON P. 105

Q

"A person is presumed innocent until proven a monster."
—DEFENSE ATTORNEY, MONSTERS' COURT

QUASIMODO

At Notre Dame, a cathedral in Paris, grotesque stone monsters squat along the ledges of the spires. Black and weathered, they have glared down on the city for centuries. Their mouths spout water from time to time when it rains, but their facial expressions never change. They are called gargoyles, and they are supposed to keep evil demons from entering the church.

It is the facade of this building that serves as the backdrop for Victor Hugo's novel *The Hunchback of Notre Dame*. The hunchback is the church bell ringer, named Quasimodo—Latin for "somehow" or "in some manner." Hunchbacked and one-eyed, Quasimodo is deaf and has barely a command of language. He walks with a limp. He is the spitting image of a certain gargoyle—they are alike as two peas in a pod. Can you recognize him among his stony look-alikes? (See: Solutions on p. 140.)

A tip for monster film freaks: Of the many Quasimodos who have graced the screen, Lon **Chaney**'s hunchback is the most wondrously ugly of them all.

"ratatatatatatatatatatatatat..."
—THE SOUND OF A MACHINE GUN

RAMBO

A special breed of monsters looks almost human, if one disregards their monstrous muscles. Take, for example, Rambo: biceps bulging and armed to the teeth, he storms the Vietnamese jungle. He bangs away wildly on his machine gun, slaughtering hundreds of people. When he finally runs out of bullets, he tosses grenades, shoots with a bow and arrow, and murders with his bare hands. Only then might he take a breather. But not for long. After Rambo's first adventure, *First Blood* (1982), comes *Rambo: First Blood Part II* (1985), and *Rambo III* (1988). Yes, you've guessed it— we're talking about the movies starring Sylvester Stallone.

Characters like Rambo call themselves human beings, yet their behavior is unworthy even of a monster. Indeed, **Frankenstein**'s monster seems like a cuddly teddy bear in comparison to such homicidal maniacs.

S

"Too many cooks spoil the monster."
—PROVERB IN NEED OF AN UPDATE

SELF-MADE MONSTERS

Dusk is falling, and your party guests are sitting around somewhat bored. No one seems to know what to do next. The time has come for you to make your move. Why not introduce your new homemade game? Just follow these simple instructions:

1. Prepare two lists: On the left, write the names of 10 dangerous household utensils or tools. On the right, list the names of 10 animals that you find creepy or that sound bizarre:

Meat Mallet	Newt
Barbed Wire	Adder
Poultry Shears	Toad
Buzz Saw	Vulture
Mousetrap	Tarantula
Pitchfork	Medusa
Cleaver	Stingray
Curling Iron	Scorpion
Soldering Iron	Lemur
Ice Pick	Gila Monster

Have you figured it out already? Right. Join a name from the first list to one from the second list and you have a marvelous new monster. For example: a meat-mallet lemur, or a cleavertoad.

2. Now make two more lists, so that these original characters will have a place to live. On the left, list 10 creepy adjectives (words that describe), and on the right, list 10 horrific places. A few suggestions:

Moss-Covered
Subterranean
Slithery
Mildewy
Oozing
Blood-Soaked
Crustaceous
Ancient
Contaminated
Cavernous

Ruins
Caves
Cemeteries
Ghost Towns
Sewer Pipes
Dungeons
Swamps
Moors
Garbage Dumps
Gorges

Yes, monsters love such places. They feel at ease in moss-covered garbage dumps, blood-soaked gorges, and subterranean cemeteries....

3. And what do these tender creatures eat? Concoct your own delicious dish:

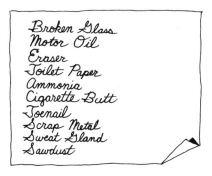

Broken Glass
Motor Oil
Eraser
Toilet Paper
Ammonia
Cigarette Butt
Toenail
Scrap Metal
Sweat Gland
Sawdust

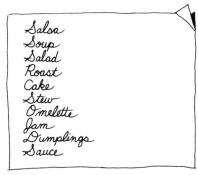

Salsa
Soup
Salad
Roast
Cake
Stew
Omelette
Jam
Dumplings
Sauce

Such gourmets! Eraser roast with toenail sauce—and for dessert, sweat-gland cake!

4. Monsters also have their particular quirks and hobbies. Try out a few of these:

Collecting
Painting
Reading about
Breeding
Cuddling
Tinkering with
Preserving
Playing Ping-Pong with

Wretched Mouth Odors
Soggy Sweat Socks
Rattling Skeletons
Clogged Drainpipes
Rotten Eggs
Dusty Spider Webs
Rat Holes
Compost

That's just how they are, the little darlings. They play Ping-Pong with rat holes and like to cuddle clogged drainpipes!

5. And now to make your game pieces: You'll need construction paper in 8 different colors. Cut out 10 cards of each color, about the size of playing cards. Write the words from one of your lists (one word per card) on all the cards of the same color. Repeat with each list of words, using a different color for each list.

6. To make a game board, use a piece of sturdy cardboard. Outline a game card 8 times around the board. In the middle, glue on or draw (see: **drawing monsters**) your favorite monster. Pile the cards from each word group face down on the spaces.

7. Now for the ghastly, horrifying game! First, create the right atmosphere (candlelight, soft tango music). Then, let each player draw one card from each pile. Allow 3 to 5 minutes for the players to think up a little story for their monster and its habits. Then have one player begin. His or her story might go something like this:

"Did you know that there's such a thing as a BUZZ-SAW TARAN-TULA? No? Well, they are very rare, almost extinct. You are most likely to find them in MILDEWY MOORS.

"Instead of teeth, they have two fast rotating, round buzz-saw blades. They love eating BROKEN GLASS SALAD with motor oil. Their table manners are excellent. They don't smack their lips or slurp. Only now and then you'll hear the annoying sound of a napkin getting stuck in a saw blade.

"I have one as a pet. It lives in the basement near the hot water heater. Sometimes, my monster CUDDLES WITH DUSTY SPIDER WEBS. When it does this, it rolls its three eyes and lets its saw blades whirl. The next time you come to my house, bring your leather work gloves with you—then you can pet my sweet friend too!"

If the other players like the story, they should not applaud. To show their enthusiasm, they may: chatter their teeth, crawl under the table, bite their nails, or exhibit their fear in any number of ways.

SPOOKY

A little monster who can't fall asleep cries: "Mommy, I'm so scared! A hideous little girl is lurking behind the curtain! She has curly hair, long eyelashes, and dimpled cheeks! And just imagine— none of her teeth are pointed, and...."

Mother monster responds soothingly, "You're just imagining things, my dear little pet bat. Try to sleep now. You know that there are no such things as little girls with curly hair...."

STAR WARS

STAR WARS:
1. The name of a program for the development of atomic space weapons, also called SDI (Strategic Defense Initiative). Launched by Ronald Reagan when he was president of the United States.
2. A 1977 film directed by George Lucas. The first in a series, it was followed by *The Empire Strikes Back* (1980) and *Return of the Jedi* (1983).

Item 1 was a bitter reality.

Item 2 is a fantastic fairy tale that takes place in the 23rd century. In it, good guys fight bad guys in ultrafast spaceships with laser swords. Princesses are saved by the heroic Jedi knights and everything comes to a happy end. A number of remarkable monsters join the cast, from all parts of the galaxy. Here are a few of them:

CHEWBACCA: Good. Big and strong. A Wookie from the planet Kazhyyt. Friend of the human hero Han Solo (good). Likes to drape himself with cartridge belts.

DARTH VADER: Super bad, downright evil. Ruler of the Deathstar. From behind his black mask, he frightens everyone with the monstrously loud sound of his own breathing. Who or what is concealed behind Darth Vader's steely exterior? A human being? A monster? Or what?

JABBA THE HUT: Bad. Ruler of the desert planet Tatooine. For this creature, sticking out its tongue is not a sign of bad manners, but of extreme concentration.

JAWAS: Semi-good. Natives of Tatooine. Jawas are only partially organic and deal in scrap metal. They ride Banthas.

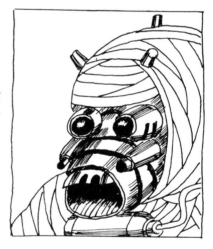

RANCOR: Bad. Jabba's favorite pet. To entertain its master, it gobbles up whatever is tossed in its direction.

SALACIOUS CRUMB: Bad. Jabba's best buddy. No further commentary needed.

YODA: Good. Has lived for more than 800 years on the swampy planet of Dagobah. Teacher of the Jedi knights. Master of "the force."

(By the way, the monster masks for *Star Wars* were created by the Uglies Corporation!)

SHE CRAWLS UNDER THE BED AND SCREAMS FOR HER MOTHER.

CONTINUED ON P.111

T

(Greek: tera = *monster)*

TERATOLOGY

How easy it seems for the ornithologists, those bird experts! They loaf lazily about in nature, from time to time raising their field glasses or turning the pages in their pretty picture books.

We teratologists, or monster specialists, on the other hand, not only have to fight our way over torturous terrain to the most remote monster nesting sites, but we also have to reckon with their extremely skittish or aggressive behavior. That is, we have to be made of sterner stuff. Prerequisites for a top-notch teratologist are: toughness, courage, lightning-quick reflexes, endurance, and—absolutely vital—a lively imagination.

Here is a list of the most basic gear you'll need:

1 MOON LOTION (see: **full moon**)
2 MIRROR (see: **basilisk**)
3 LASER-BEAM DISINTEGRATION PISTOL (see: **aliens**)
4 CONSECRATED WAFERS, CRUCIFIX, GARLIC (see: **Dracula, vampires**)
5 WILD ROSE, SCALPEL, HAMMER, WOODEN STAKE, IRON STAKE (see: **vampires**)
6 LIGHTER (the iron stake has to be glowing-hot—see: **vampires**)
7 SHOVEL (for burying **vampires** at crossroads)
8 FLYSWATTER (see: **The Fly, Godzilla**)
9 FINS, DIVING GOGGLES, SNORKEL (see: **Loch Ness**)
10 **3-D** GLASSES
11 INSECTICIDE (see: **The Fly, Godzilla**)
12 BICYCLE (see: **griffins**)
13 WAX (to protect ears from the song of the Sirens—see: **monsters of Greek mythology**)
14 GAMMA-RAY REVOLVER (see: **Hulk**)
15 HARPOON (see: **Jaws**)
16 UNDERWATER CAMERA (see: **Loch Ness**)
17 BOTTLE OF FORTIFYING BEVERAGE (see: **Phantom**)
18 KNITTING NEEDLE (see: **mechanical monsters**)

19 LIPSTICK (to attract **King Kong**)
20 DEODORANT (to repel **ogres:** they love the smell of human flesh)
21 FIRE EXTINGUISHER (for use against fire-spitting **dragons**)
22 SPONGE (to erase the *e* in *emeth*—see: **golem**)
23 WASTEBASKET (see: **bogeymonster**)
24 CRAMPONS, PICK, ROPE, CLIMBER'S HELMET (see: **Yeti**)
25 MEDICAL INSURANCE CARD (needed by born heroes—see: **fear**)
26 LAMP (see: **dragons, golem, mummies, Phantom**)
27 CROWBAR (to open tombs and coffins)
28 ID (required by law)
29 MOONGLASSES (see: **full moon**)
30 *MONSTER MANUAL* (always at hand anyway)

THEATER

You're not into theater? You can't sit still for two hours in a tuxedo or evening gown? Okay, then, why don't you stage a play yourself? The *Monster Manual* team has written, especially for you and your friends, a theatrically effective monster sketch that can be performed at parties or holiday festivities. Roaring applause is guaranteed!

You'll need two actors: Dress yourselves monsterlike—exactly how is up to you. Try flippers, slippers, ski boots, bathing suits, wigs, goggles, toilet paper (see: **mummies**), crash helmets, bathing caps, gas masks, raincoats, bedsheets, balloons, pantyhose, pajamas, neckties, bowties, beekeeper masks.... A trip to a thrift shop can fire your imagination.

You'll need a stage: Paint windows, doors, balconies, etc., on different-sized cardboard boxes. Create a city scene with them. Add some toy cars, dolls, and action figures to the town. In one of the houses, place a battery-operated cassette player. Above the city, hang a sign that says: "CHICAGO, 2002, MIDNIGHT."

You'll need a script: But you don't need to learn it by heart. It doesn't matter what you say, as long as it sounds harsh, incomprehensible, and monstrous. It's *how* you say your lines that's important.

The title of the play is:

MONSTERS ARE BIG-HEARTED, AREN'T THEY?
or
ARE MONSTERS BAD BABY-SITTERS?

The stage is empty, except for the miniature city. From the distance, heavy steps, angry grunts, and roars can be heard. From each side of the stage, two huge monsters enter the city. In their savagery or clumsiness, they trample houses, pick up cars and people, and toss them away after having sniffed or tasted them. The monsters growl in annoyance or purr contentedly. Monster A picks up the house in which the cassette player is hidden.

Monster A (to Monster B): Aybeeceedee, eeefgeeaitch i jaykayelemenopee.

Monster B (grabs the house from A and states sternly): Cuearesteeu, veedoubleuex whyzee! Aybeeceedee! Eeefgeeaitch!

Monster A (takes back the house, angry): Ijaykayelemen opee cueares? Teeuveedoubleu? EX! WHY! ZEE!

Monster B (grabs back the house, screams): AY! BEE! CEE!... Deeeefgeeaitchijaykayelemenopeecuear-esteeuveedoubleuexwhyzee!

Monster A (roars indignantly): AAAAAAY, beebeebeebee, ceeceeceecee! Deeeeef. Geeaitch i jaykay? Elelememenenoopeepeecuecue!!!

Monster B (screams madly): ARARARARARARARARARARARA-RARARARAR! ESESESESESESESESES! TEETEETEETEETEETEETEE! Uuuuuuuuuuuuuuuuuuuuuuuuu! Veedoubleuexwhyzee!!!!!

There's a brawl. The monsters try first to impress one another by taking up all sorts of fighting positions, then they shove each other around a bit, and finally they fly at each other's throats. More houses are knocked over, chaos ensues. The house over which they have been arguing is used as a weapon. (The audience shouldn't notice when one of the monsters pushes the start button on the hidden cassette player.) Cries of a baby come from the house. The monsters suddenly stop fighting, listen, look inside the house, and then look at each other.

Monster A (holds a finger to its lips and whispers):
Aybeeceedeeeefgeeaitch? Ijaykayel? EM!

Monster B (a finger at its lips, answers softly):
Enopeecuear! Esteeuveedoubleu....

Monster A (quietly and disapprovingly):
Exwhyzeeaybee? Ceedeeeefgee!

Monster B (apologetically): aitchijaykay...
elemenoooooooo. Peecue.

Monster A (smiles forgivingly): AR!
Esteeuveedoubleu. Exwhyzee.

In the meantime, the baby's cries have become softer and then they stop completely. The two monsters carefully look inside the house, put it down tenderly, and tiptoe off in opposite directions. Before they leave, they turn around and wave good-bye to each other.

Monster B: Aybeecee!
Monster A: Exwhyzee!

(Curtain)

If the stage is now bombarded with tomatoes or rotten eggs, that's fine. Nothing could be more appropriate after a monster play. However, if thundering applause breaks loose, return hand in hand to the stage and take a bow. If there are cries of "Encore," then recite the alphabet one more time.

So why are you still sitting around? Get to work! Nothing ventured, nothing maimed!

GLORP SQUEALS WITH PLEASURE.

(CONTINUED ON P. 115)

OKAY! NOW IT'S YOUR TURN TO BE AFRAID!

3-D

A few decades ago, kids your age saw some pretty weird movie presentations. Audiences sat—frightened out of their wits—wearing cardboard glasses that had one red and one blue lens. Without these glasses, an audience saw nothing but a mess of colors and forms on the screen. With the glasses, viewers shrieked with terror.

It wasn't the fishlike appearance of Gill-Man and his slippery evildoings that wreaked such havoc, but the feeling that the monster would climb down from the screen. And the rocks and boulders that he flung seemed about to smash directly into the theater.

3-D (three-dimensionality) was the cause of this uncanny experience. Normally, films appear two-dimensional, or flat. A three-dimensional effect gives the impression of depth. The effect is achieved by stereoscopy: two cameras, placed about two inches (the distance between the eyes) apart, are used to film a scene. The two films are then projected over one another simultaneously. The red-and blue-lensed glasses make it possible to see each frame as one three-dimensional picture. It's as simple as that.

You can make 3-D pictures yourself. For the exclusive, inside information, turn to page 114.

Make Your Own 3-D Glasses

1. Place a sheet of tracing paper over the illustration of the two monsters on page 113.

2. Trace the top monster with a red pencil.

3. Now place this drawing over the bottom monster so that the outer frames line up. Trace the second monster with a blue pencil.

4. Cut frames for your glasses from a piece of cardboard. Use red and blue see-through candy wrappers for lenses.

5. Your red-and-blue picture now looks three-dimensional! The longer you look, the stronger the effect. If you find it difficult, then you are astigmatic* or a cyclops (see: **monsters of Greek mythology**).

6. Try to design your own 3-D monsters! Draw a red line to the left of a blue line, and this part of your monster will look like it is in the foreground. Draw a red line to the right of a blue line to make it look like it is in the background. With a bit of patience and a few tries, your monsters will leap off the page too. Have fun!

RED   LEFT

BLUE   RIGHT

HANDLE   3-D GLASSES 1:1

*Ask your eye doctor!

For whatever reason, 3-D movies quickly went out of fashion. Maybe it was because the glasses were uncomfortable, or because the quality of the technology wasn't great.

The most famous 3-D film is *House of Wax* (1953), in which a mad scientist dips dead—or sometimes living—bodies into wax and then puts them on display. When the museum catches fire, the wax coatings gradually melt, producing a spectacular cinematic moment. Yet the director of the film couldn't even appreciate the effects. André de Toth had just one good eye, so he couldn't see three-dimensionally at all! If his choice of occupation raised any eyebrows, de Toth reminded his fans of Beethoven. The famous composer lost his hearing, but he didn't let a disability affect his career either.

GLORP QUAKES AND SHAKES...   AND WAILS HIS DEEPEST OOOOOOOO.

CONTINUED ON P. 126

V

*"A clove of garlic a day
keeps these monsters away."*
—ANOTHER WISE OLD TRANSYLVANIAN SAYING

VAMPIRES

Now please don't let this frighten you terribly: Vampires exist! In Central and South America, a small bat (*Desmodus rotundus*) feeds on the blood of larger animals, usually cattle. It punctures the skin of a sleeping cow, for example, with its tiny sharp front teeth. It doesn't suck the animal's blood, but funnels the blood into its throat with its tongue. It needs, at most, about two ounces of blood per day—a mere drop. So it doesn't bother the cow much. The danger with vampire bats is that they may carry diseases, such as rabies. Humans are not usually bothered by these bats, however, except in tales of fiction.

You may rest assured that *human* vampires don't exist! You were pretty sure of this all along, anyway, weren't you? Yet we have occasionally run into a vampire-related death. As recently as 1973, a man was found dead in his New York apartment, having choked during the night on a clove of garlic he had in his mouth. Garlic hung all over his bedroom. There was even a clove wedged into the keyhole. Vampires did not cause his death, but his fear of them did!

HISTORICAL INFORMATION

Vampirism is a recurring theme in the legends, fairy tales, and superstitions of almost all peoples on earth. The most famous vampire of all is Count **Dracula.** But vampires have come in all shapes, sizes, and blood groups.

Folktales and Beliefs about Vampires

What follows is a summary of the habits, strengths, weaknesses, likes, and dislikes of this dreadful brood. And since we are leaving the realm of reason and entering the realm of horrible fantasy, some of the following statements contradict each other or are completely illogical.

1. Vampires are not dead.
2. Vampires are not alive.
3. Vampires are undead.
4. Vampires feed on human blood.
5. Vampires bite the throats of their victims with two pointed fangs.
6. Vampires look puffy and bloated after their meals.
7. Vampires look years younger after they have drunk fresh blood.
8. Vampires prefer their loved ones as victims.
9. Vampires prefer the opposite sex as victims.
10. A person who has been bitten once craves to be bitten again.

11. Vampires are faithful to their victims, until they are parted by death.

12. Vampire victims die from excessive blood loss.

13. People who have been bitten by a vampire become vampires themselves after death.

14. People who have been bitten by a vampire do not turn into vampires after death *if* the vampire that bit them is killed before the victim dies.

15. Vampires communicate telepathically* with their victims.

16. Vampires have no power over people who carry a consecrated wafer or a cross.

17. Vampires hate the smell of garlic.

18. Vampires don't have a shadow, nor can they be seen in a mirror.

19. Vampires are pale, with reddish eyes and moist crimson lips.

20. Vampires have only one nostril.

*telepathy = thought transference

21. Vampires have hair on the palms of their hands and long, pointed fingernails.

22. Vampires have a pointed needle at the end of their tongues.

23. Vampires give off a moldy, rotten stench.

24. Vampires can transform themselves only at dawn or dusk.

25. Vampires can transform themselves at any time during the night.

26. Vampires can transform themselves into wolves, dogs, and bats.

27. Vampires have the ability to find hidden treasures.

28. Vampires have power over dogs, rats, wolves, bats, and the weather.

29. Female vampires are meaner than male vampires.

30. Vampires can live to be more than 1,000 years old.

31. Vampires can climb up smooth walls.

32. Vampires can enter a house only if they are invited. After having been asked once, they may enter whenever they like.

33. Vampires cannot cross flowing water.

34. Vampires sleep in coffins.

35. A vampire cannot leave its coffin when a spray of wild roses lies on top of it.

36. A **werewolf** becomes a vampire after its death.

37. People who commit suicide become vampires, if they are not buried at a crossroads.

38. Vampires die on exposure to daylight.

39. Vampires don't die from daylight, they merely become weak.

40. A vampire can be killed only if a hard wooden stake or a glowing-hot iron stake is thrust through its heart, nailing it to the bottom of its coffin.

41. Vampires can be killed by having their heads cut off. Their mouths then have to be stuffed with garlic.

42. Vampires who have taken on the form of a wolf can be killed by a silver bullet that has been dipped in holy water.

43. Very old vampires disintegrate into dust when they are killed.

44. A dead vampire who does not distintegrate into dust has to be buried at a crossroads.

45. Vampirism is a form of penance for one's sins.

46. Vampires want to be relieved of their suffering, but they are forced to resist all temptations to relieve themselves.

47. Vampires celebrate their most important holiday on November 30.

48. Vampires celebrate their most important holiday on April 26.

49. Vampires exist.

50. Vampires don't exist.

THE MODERN VAMPIRE

And now, exclusively for *Monster Manual:* an interview with Countess Wampyr!

For the first time ever, and through more effort than words can express, the *Monster Manual* reporter team was successful in persuading one of the last living female vampires, Countess Wampyr, to give an interview. She granted it only on the condition that neither her picture nor her address be publicized. Here is the team's report:

Dusk was just falling and it was quite foggy when our team arrived at the countess's villa. Bloodwort, nightshade plants, mistletoe, and other parasitic vegetation grew wild in the large yard in front of the house. The countess, a pale, stately woman of indeterminable age, opened the door herself and ushered us in.

The rooms were large and dimly lit, the furniture old and expensive. A musky odor hung in the air. We took a seat in the library. The countess answered our questions most readily and was full of spirit, although she kept a respectful distance. Her voice was deep, and when the word blood *was mentioned, she gently licked her lips. When she laughed, she discreetly covered her mouth with her hand.*

Monster Manual: Countess, our knowledge of vampires is quite meager and often contradictory. Nonetheless, one thing seems to be certain: vampires drink blood.

Countess: Naturally. I personally prefer type AB blood, Rh-negative. If possible, from non-smokers and nonalcoholics. But tastes differ. For example, an acquaintance of mine, a very sensitive gourmet, swears by slightly anemic blood.

"I PREFER TYPE AB BLOOD, RH-NEGATIVE."

MM: How much blood do you require daily?

C: Well, a small glass or two. Only on special occasions do I consume more. But then I'm sure not to touch a drop the next day. One does have to watch one's figure!

MM: You mentioned a "small glass." According to the reports we have read about vampires....

C: I understand what you're getting at. You believe that we vampires still suck blood from the throats of our victims. Now, really! We are approaching the 21st century! Do you still eat with your fingers? Honestly, you humans! I have an account at the blood bank, and I withdraw just as much as I need for one month. I store the extra bottles in the cellar at the proper temperature. It's no problem at all, in this age of blood transfusions. It's also a question of hygiene. You wouldn't believe the number of humans who run about with dirty collars and unwashed necks! It makes me lose my appetite to even think of them!

MM: But Count Dracula....

C: Please, don't mention his name in my presence! That coarse, Transylvanian hillbilly with his unappetizing table manners and his perverse traveling habits has given our species a terrible reputation! He is a true black sheep among vampires.

MM: We're quite sorry, Countess, we didn't intend to—

C: Say no more! It's your fault, too—the fault of all writers and filmmakers. The atrocious crimes committed by this sick drunk have been shouted from housetop to housetop for decades, and since humans love to generalize, all vampires must be like he is! Yet I don't compare all of humanity with, let's say…Jack the Ripper. I beg your pardon, if I've gotten a bit emotional, but this matter has to be settled, once and for all!

MM: Your eating habits lead us to conclude that you are quite wealthy. People claim that vampires know how to find hidden treasures.

C: Come, come! Your romantic notions are quite comical. Do I truly look like I need to dig for treasures with a pick and shovel? You know, I am—I don't mind telling you—almost 600 years old. Relatively young for a vampire, yet old enough to be able to turn it into profit. I make millions on the art and antique markets. Here, for example—take this small painting. I attained it in 1480 from a certain Hieronymus **Bosch,** for, let's say…for the value of a few drops of blood. If I were to put it up for auction today, I would be able to buy thousands of gallons of blood with the price it would bring. And don't forget all the jewelry and coins! Even simple every-day objects from the Middle Ages bring in horrendous prices nowadays. One needs only to be able to wait long enough. And I've got all the time in the world.

MM: How do you explain that you have been able to attain such a ripe old age? Oh, excuse me—what I mean is, how do you explain your youthful appearance at, er, a *relatively* advanced age—by human standards?

"MY HOBBIES ARE TRAINING BATS AND BREEDING LEECHES."

C: Leisurely nighttime flights—no matter what the weather, sleeping with the coffin lid open, and having a few hobbies. My hobbies are, by the way, training bats to perform tricks and breeding leeches.

MM: Countess Wampyr, I hope you'll not be offended if we bring up a theme that you probably find quite revolting: garlic.

C: But of course not! Garlic doesn't bother me one bit. I couldn't care less about garlic. It's good you brought it up, too. I'm always interested in doing away with people's prejudices. Where people got the idea that vampires loathe garlic, I can only guess! Perhaps it came about because many humans like the taste of garlic. The smell of garlic only disturbs those who don't eat it. Instead of being considerate of others and eating less garlic, garlic-eaters spread the idea that garlic is good against vampires. They had found a reason to thus indulge themselves. Or something along these lines. Haven't your psychologists unearthed the truth yet?

MM: To conclude, one more ticklish matter: we humans fear vampires because they rob us of a very important life fluid—blood. When you drink your daily little

"BLOOD, BLOOD, BLOOD!"

glass, aren't you sometimes troubled by slight pangs of guilt?

C: Young man, let me clear this up right here and now. You, as a human, have no right to question my morals! Especially where blood is concerned! What is a ridiculously little glass of blood compared to all the blood that humanity has shed? The blood from wars, the blood from bombings, the blood that has drenched battlefields, the blood from revolutions, the blood from the destruction of whole nations. Everything humans touch turns to blood, blood, blood! Blood that cannot be measured in small glasses, not even in gallons. And you dare to accuse us vampires? Oh, talking doesn't help. I feel more like...(smack)..like....

MM: Er, we thank you for the interview, Countess.

Toward the end of the interview, the Countess's eyes took on a red shimmer and her incisors appeared to become longer and more pointed. These signs and her irritated state led us to quickly pack our equipment and depart.

For more on the subject of vampires, see: **Dracula** and **Nosferatu.** You may also want to read Deborah and James Howe's *Bunnicula.* A particularly amusing vampire movie is Roman Polanski's *The Fearless Vampire Killers* (1967).

HE CRAWLS UNDER THE BED AND SCREAMS FOR
HIS MOTHER. (CONTINUED ON P. 134)

W

"Never torture an animal for fun—
it might be a monster."
—UZBEK PROVERB

WEREWOLVES

There's a full moon. In a lonesome hut in the woods, a man paces back and forth restlessly. Suddenly, thick, bushy hair sprouts on his hands and face, then all over his body. His teeth grow pointed and sharp. His fingernails and toenails turn into claws. With an angry growl, this being—no longer human, but not yet animal—rips off its clothes. Finally, the transformation is complete: the man has become a huge wolf with gnashing teeth. Craving human flesh, the monster creeps from the hut. With a mournful howl to the moon, it sets off in search of food....

The creature in this story is a werewolf, of course. After its bloody meal, and when the moon sets, it will turn back into a human being.

In the ancient ruin of a 13th-century North Siberian monastery, archaeologists have uncovered a yellowed fragment from a book about werewolves. It shall be presented here for the first time, exclusively for Monster Fans. We're sorry that we didn't find more, but it is, most likely, for the best:

Blynded soul, who dareth to cast a glance behynd the mystery, let here be revealed whych magycal powers and black sorcery thou shalt use to transform thyself ynto a terrible werewolf. Consyder thy step deep yn thy soul, before evyl forces wynneth power over thee and thou regret thyne unfortunate decysyon. Thou must realyze: thou shalt return no more!

At full moon on a Fryday the 13th, go to an elevated clearyng yn the forest from whych thou can hear the howls of the wolves!

Mark at mydnyght wyth ground wolfbones a cyrcle of three feet yn dyameter. Yn the center of the cyrcle lyght a fyre under a sylver pot yn whych thou hath placed toad eyes, gryffyn feathers, snake poyson, and the droppyngs of a basylysk.

Smear thy body wyth the fynyshed broth and hang a bloody wolfskyn over thy shoulders.

Look torward the East and speak the magyc charm whych runneth so:

HISTORICAL INFORMATION

Tales about werewolves are quite old. In one Greek legend, King Lycaon is turned into a people-eating wolf when he enrages Zeus, king of the gods.

Pliny, a Roman author, wrote that people who had been sacrificed to the gods turned into hungry wolves. They were released from the spell after nine years, but only if they followed a strict diet that excluded even one tasty morsel of human flesh.

Wolves and werewolves have also haunted our superstitions. It has been said, for example, that people turn into werewolves if they wear a wolf hide or a belt made from the skin of a person who was lynched. Or, some legends say, the ability to turn into a werewolf is hereditary. There's the belief that when a werewolf takes on a human form, it turns its skin inside out, so that its fur cannot be seen.

In the Middle Ages, people actually believed in the existence of werewolves. People who had eyebrows that grew together over their noses, hair on their hands, or long middle fingers were considered werewolves. As with witches, werewolves were hunted down, prosecuted, and burned at the stake. Between 1520 and 1630, 30,000 "werewolves" were sentenced to death in France alone. Some of these people were even skinned, to expose the fur they were supposedly concealing.

Looking back on this, we might say that the real werewolves of the Middle Ages were the blood-hungry judges—as well as everyone who took part in the wolf hunts, howling along with the pack.

WEREWOLVES IN THE MOVIES

Werewolf movies are quite common. Especially popular are those in which the werewolf has a showdown with another famous monster, such as *Frankenstein Meets the Wolf Man* (1943). The monsters growl, hiss, bite, and scratch. Blood spatters, and sparks fly. Even the moon pales noticeably as it quickly hides behind dark clouds.

The most famous werewolf was played by Lon **Chaney**, Jr., son of the famous silent film star. Like his father, Chaney was subjected to some unusually long **makeup** sessions. His transformation into the wolf man was no exception. It took 6 hours to glue all the hairs to his face and 2 hours to remove them. Then it took almost 24 hours for the famous metamorphosis to be filmed. Once again, it was the makeup artist Jack B. Pierce (see: **Frankenstein**) who was responsible for this marvelous feat.

"Don't make a monster out of a molehill."
—GOOD ADVICE FROM DR. X

X HAS THE ANSWER

When someone has a delicate question about monsters, Dr. X (a walking 48-volume encyclopedia) has the answer. His advice on the most difficult of problems never fails, either. Here is a sample of Dr. X's correspondence with Monster Fans in need of advice:

Wolfgang, 11 years old: On full-moon nights, hairs suddenly grow on my face and my teeth become long and pointed. Am I in need of a doctor?
Dr. X says: No, not a doctor. They taste awful—like medicine. A florist or a cook is better.

Sandra, 15 years old: I have fallen in love with a darling **zombie.** Is such a being capable of returning my deeply felt emotions?
Dr. X says: Yes, but only if you suffer from leprosy or oversized pimples.

A worried mother, 45 years old: My 10-year-old daughter walks in her sleep. On her nightly outings, she climbs on the roof, howls at the moon, and tries to catch bats. I can hardly sleep for fear of not waking up in time to prevent her from these dangerous undertakings. I'm absolutely desperate. What is your advice?
Dr. X says: Scatter thumbtacks on the floor around your daughter's bed. If she climbs out of bed, she will certainly wake up.

Bessie, 10 years old: My mother is incredibly strict. Recently, she has tried to ruin my harmless walks in my sleep by scattering thumbtacks around my bed. I can hardly sleep for fear of waking up with thumbtacks in the soles of my feet. What should I do?
Dr. X says: Wear sturdy walking shoes to bed.

Joe, 16 years old: To protect myself against monsters, should I practice judo, karate, or freestyle wrestling?
Dr. X says: Running, dear Joe. You should practice running!

Shane, 14 years old: On weekends, I like to get together with a few **aliens** at the YMCA. My parents think my alien friends have a bad influence on me and won't let me go there anymore. Do I have to accept this?
Dr. X says: Unfortunately, you do! But maybe you can persuade them to change their minds. Try to make your parents realize how old-fashioned they are behaving, and that they shouldn't object to your friends just because they are different.

Frankenstein's monster, 172 years old: Humans often tease me about my big feet. Do you think this is fair?
Dr. X says: No. I think it is truly nasty to laugh at your two left feet, clunky and comically cornered as they are.

Anne, 9 years old: On Sunday, an **ogre** is coming to dinner. What do you recommend serving?

Dr. X says: Yourself, little Anne. Ogres aren't fussy.

If you have any pressing questions (Does **King Kong** play Ping-Pong? Does **Hulk** have hemorrhoids?), then write to:

Dr. X
13 Nightshade Lane
Gallowsville, Leucomania

Y

"Yetiooleeoh!"
—YODELLER FROM THE HIMALAYAS

YETI

What, you've never seen it? Then you probably live in a densely populated area. The yeti, or the Abominable Snowman, loves the outdoor life—in inaccessible mountain ranges and vast unexplored forests. Its footprints have often been found and photographed (although the quality of the photos is pretty much like those photos of Nessie—see: **Loch Ness**). Reports of yeti sightings by mountain climbers, explorers, and adventurous mushroom hunters appear from time to time in the newspapers.

Some years ago, a man exhibited such a creature (frozen in a block of ice) at all sorts of sideshows and fairs. He called it "The Iceman of Minnesota." When reporters and scientists began to show interest, however, both snowman and showman vanished into thin air.

WANTED: **YETI** (HIMALAYAS)

ALIAS XUEREN (CHINA), ALIAS HIBAGON (JAPAN), ALIAS CHUCHUNAA (SIBERIA), ALIAS YOWIE (AUSTRALIA), ALIAS ALMAS (CAUCASUS), ALIAS CHEMOSIT (AFRICA), ALIAS SASQUATCH (CANADA), ALIAS BIGFOOT (USA), ALIAS MARICOXI (SOUTH AMERICA)

←—— SHOULDER WIDTH 5'11" ——→   ←— 10" —→

HEIGHT 6'7"–9'10"

FOOTPRINT

REPORT RELEVANT INFO TO THE SUPER-MARKET TABLOID OF YOUR CHOICE. REWARD! (ONE-YEAR SUBSCRIP-TION ABSOLUTELY FREE!)

Here are some explanations for the existence of this mysterious monster. Which explanation do you think is most likely?

The yeti is:
1) an unknown kind of monkey
2) a hermit who hates making the long journey to the hairdresser's
3) a descendant of a prehistoric race of humans (*Gigantopithecus*)
4) a bear (when a bear walks in a certain way, its footprints can resemble those of an oversized human)
5) a product of overanxious, nervous, or drunk imaginations
6) a jogging heavyweight boxer, training under extreme conditions in a fur coat
7) an invention of people who want to get their names in the newspapers
8) an **alien** who became stranded on earth when its spaceship had engine trouble

DAWN BREAKS, THE MOON WANES. GLORP SAYS GOOD-BYE.
(CONTINUED ON P. 139)

YUCK, GAG, PUKE

Now hold on tight and get ready for the biggest disappointment of your life: Monsters have to go to school too!

Just like you, monsters of school age have to put up with too-long school days, stuffy classrooms, dreadful tests, unbearable lessons, oppressive homework, unfair teachers, fierce principals—in other words, with typical school stress. Of course, monster pupils study different subjects than you do. While your brain sizzles over impossible math problems, monster kids' jaws ache from hours of baring their teeth (a requirement even for toothless monsters). And they don't like homework either: it's no fun to have to uproot 50 trees or to prepare for a poison-spitting test, when you'd rather be at the garbage dump playing spitball with your friends.

If you are interested, however, monster schools can be attended by humans, too. To qualify, you not only have to have been kicked out of your own school for bad behavior, but you have to have been kicked so hard that you've landed on the dark side of the moon. That's where the School of Monstrology is located.

To give you a notion of its scholastic program, here is Monster Glorp's report card. Glorp was not exactly a model monster pupil. Nevertheless, as we know, he did turn out to be a quite decent and proper monster.

School of Monstrology
Jules Verne Crater
Moon [darkside]

Report Card
for

George Glorp, the Horror of Humanity
[name]   [epithet]
born 1528 in Swampomania
In the school year 1539–40, this pupil
attended the 3rd grade in the department
of Mud Monsters and received the
following grades in the following subjects:

Subjects	Grades
scratching, biting, strangling	B+
fire-eating, fire-breathing	D
blood-sucking [for vampires only]	–
stinking	A
oozing slime, slobbering, foaming	A–
rolling eyes, baring teeth	B
scary and threatening behavior	A
conjuring up thunderstorms	F
concocting poisonous brews	–
changing form	F
elective: mud slinging	A

(left margin, top group) subjects
(left margin, bottom group) main subjects

continued on back

continued from front

language	cursing	B−
	wheezing, rattling	A
	recitation of magic formulas	D+
	foreign language: Gruntonish	no grade
music	roaring, howling, screeching	A
	singing at the moon	C
	skeletal percussion	absent
sports	uprooting trees	A
	trampling houses	B
	swimming in hydrochloric acid	—*
	mud fights	A

*no evaluation possible, allergic to acid

This pupil is — eligible by the skin of his teeth to move up into the 4th grade.

June 13, 1540

Teacher   Principal

Key to grades: A = ultra-monstrous, B = phantasmic, C = ogreish, D = lycanthropal, F = beastly

Z

"To be or zom bie"
—WILLIAM SHAKES

ZOMBIES

At the entrance to Hell, a sign reads: "Closed due to overpopulation." The dead disappointedly turn around and drag their feet back to earth.

It was such an unfortunate situation, most likely, that flooded the world with these walking corpses in George Romero's films *Night of the Living Dead* (1968), and *Dawn of the Dead* (1979).

All in trances, they stagger about—slowly, with expressionless faces, lacking all willpower, mute. They see nothing, hear nothing, and feel nothing. One of them falls down a flight of stairs. Others trample over it as if they are sleepwalking. It gets up again. Its clothes are torn, one arm is missing, an eye dangles down to its jaw. It totters on, leaving a trail of blood behind. The zombies' instincts lead them to the last living humans. The zombies find the nourishment they need: human flesh.

The humans defend themselves desperately. To destroy a zombie, they must shoot it directly in the forehead. Ammunition runs low, and the zombies multiply rapidly. The doors to Hell are no longer closed, but wide open. All kinds of creatures swarm up to earth. Is this the end of humanity?

Of course not! George Romero has more episodes up his sleeve, as do countless other moviemakers. Monster Fans everywhere can rest in peace.

MERRILY GROWLING A TUNE, GLORP MAKES HIS WAY HOME.
(CONTINUED ON P.142)

SOLUTIONS

DRACULA

The author's 10 slipups are these:

The NEW MOON (1) casts neither bizarre shadows nor any other kind of shadow.

Dracula is not a BARON (2), but rather a count.

In such circles, SUNTANNED FACES (3) are not exactly "in."

GREEN PLAID (4)! His cape is black, lined with red silk.

A VULTURE (5) is also quite scary, but a bat's more like it.

The TRANSIBERIAN (6) is a train. Dracula comes from Transylvania.

Garlic, not ONIONS (7), wards off vampires, not MOTHS (8).

CANDY (9) might be a temptation for us mortals. Vampires definitely stick to blood.

Dracula prefers the scrawniest necks to the most appetizing TOES (10).

MINI-MONSTERS

The *Sesame Street* Muppets, clockwise from center are: Oscar the Grouch (in garbage can), Grover, Bert, The Count, Cookie Monster, and Ernie.

QUASIMODO

a) You couldn't find Quasimodo? Don't worry. The smartest of **teratologists** have been brooding over this problem for years—without success.

b) What, you recognized Quasimodo? Fantastagargoylastic! You are the first to do so, and shall remain the only one. Have yourself entered in the *Guinness Book of Records!*

CONTINUED ON P. 144